A SHAMBHALA THRESHOLD BOOK

Jewels of Remembrance

A Daybook of Spiritual Guidance Containing 365 Selections From the Wisdom of

MEVLÂNA JALÂLUDDIN

RUMI

Selected and Translated by
Camille and Kabir Helminski

SHAMBHALA
Boston & London
2000

SHAMBHALA PUBLICATIONS, INC.
Horticultural Hall
300 Massachusetts Avenue
Boston, Massachusetts 02115
www.shambhala.com

Published by arrangement with Threshold Books

9 8 7 6 5 4 3 2 1

FIRST SHAMBHALA EDITION
Printed in the United States of America
♾ This edition is printed on acid-free paper that meets the American National Standards Institute Z39.48 Standard.
Distributed in the United States by Random House, Inc., and in Canada by Random House of Canada Ltd

Library of Congress Cataloging-in-Publication Data
Jalal al-Din Rumi, Maulana, 1207–1273
[Masnavi. English. Selections]
Jewels of remembrance: a daybook of spiritual guidance: containing 365 selections from the wisdom of ... Rumi/selected and translated by Camille and Kabir Helminski.
p. cm.
Includes bibliographical references and index.
ISBN 1–570–62524–7 (cloth)
1. Sufi poetry, Persian—Translations into English. I. Title.
II. Helminski, Camille Adams, 1951– III. Helminski, Kabir, 1947–
PK6481.M8 E5213 2000
891′.5511 21—dc21 99–046049

Contents

PREFACE: *Jewels of Remembrance*
CAMILLE HELMINSKI
VII

INTRODUCTION: *Under the Light of Mevlâna*
KABIR HELMINSKI
XI

SELECTIONS
1

INDEX
197

Preface

Jewels of Remembrance

Throughout the intricate tales of his *Mathnawi*, Mevlâna Jalâluddin Rumi scatters pearls and jewels of wisdom and remembrance—words that catch the light and reflect it to our souls. When it is really heard, one word can make a world of difference. A world that once was dark becomes light and expands; new meanings open and a new world of relationship becomes possible. This is the invitation Mevlâna extends to us—to see the Light of Love behind the light of this world. He encourages us to open to that Light which truly shimmers all around us, and within us, if we would open our eyes and hearts to see. Often he tells us that it is this Light that is our true nourishment.

You who are kept in pawn to food,
you can be free if you suffer yourself to be weaned.
Truly in hunger there is abundant nourishment:
search after it diligently and cherish the hope of finding it.
Feed on the Light, be like the eye,
be in harmony with the angels, O best of humankind.
Like the Angel, make glorification of God your sustenance.

[V, 295-298]

And there is no living creature on earth
but depends for its sustenance on God.

[Qur'an Surah Hud 11:6]

Within the Sufi tradition, the human being is considered the representative of God on earth. It is when the fine and subtle qualities of the Divine shine through the human being, that one begins to fulfill the potential of his or her creation. Though the qualities of the Divine are infinite, within the Sufi tradition, there are "Ninety-Nine Names" which are most often recognized. Among the qualities reflected in the verses here are those of truth, beauty, generosity, forgiveness, strength, compassion, purity, gratitude, and patience—always merciful patience, for as Mevlâna says, "Patience is the key to joy."

When Adam became the theater of Divine inspiration and love,
his rational soul revealed to him *the knowledge of the Names*[1]
His tongue, reading from the page of his heart,
recited the name of everything that is.
Through his inward vision his tongue
divulged the qualities of each;
for each it bestowed an appropriate name.
Nine hundred years Noah walked in the straight way,
and everyday he preached a new sermon.
His ruby lip drew its eloquence from the precious jewel
that is within the hearts of prophets. . . .
He had not learned to preach from pouring over commentaries;
no, he learned from the fountain of revelations and the spirit—
from the wine that is so potent that when it is quaffed
the water of speech gushes from the mouth of the dumb,
and the new-born child becomes an eloquent divine
and, like the Messiah, recites words of ripened wisdom.

[VI, 2648-2656]

---

[1] Qur'an: Surah Al-Baqarah (The Cow), 2:29.

Mevlâna Jalâluddin Rumi spoke from beyond time, from an eternal moment, so that in this moment, seven hundred years later, we can hear his words and immediately take them to heart as though no time or space separates us. It is as though we are listening to the voice of a friend who is able to put into words the yearning of our souls, and so make it comprehensible to our minds.

Continually, Mevlâna offers us an antidote to the intense isolation which so many people in the Western world have come to feel: he calls us to return, to shift our focus from the individual to the eternal whole, the Essence of all that is, by whatever name one may wish to call it. Mevlâna encourages us to dissolve our separative, particular individuality within the ocean of our Source. He reassures us that it is Love that is seeking us. He calls us to accept that we are loved, and to recognize the immense treasure we gain when we open to the Love of our Creator.

Listen, O drop, give yourself up without regret,
and in exchange gain the Ocean.
Listen, O drop, bestow upon yourself this honor,
and in the arms of the Sea be secure.
Who indeed should be so fortunate?
An Ocean wooing a drop!
In God's name, in God's name, sell and buy at once!
Give a drop, and take this Sea full of pearls.

[IV, 2619-2622]

The "jewels" included here are excerpted from Book III through Book VI of the *Mathnâwi*, often referred to as the Qur'an in the Persian tongue. Perhaps more within this volume than within the earlier companion volume, *Rumi: Daylight*, which contained selections from Books I and II, it will become apparent to the reader the extent to which Mevlâna drew nourishment from the Qur'an and the traditions of Islam. Many of the verses gathered here refer to verses in the Qur'an or to sayings of the Prophet Muhammad (peace and blessings upon him).

It is sometimes not recognized by many who are drawn to the immediacy of Rumi's vision, how much that vision was the fruit of a tree long growing in the soil of Islam. Many people in the West may view Rumi as something of an iconoclast, who whirled away in ecstasy after his meeting with the "wild man," Shams of Tabriz. If they explore Mevlâna's works more extensively, they might be surprised to discover how deeply connected he remained throughout his life to the Islamic roots from which both he and Shams drew immense nourishment. Yet the deeper Mevlâna went, the more he became an exponent of universal love, an open presence of unremitting acceptance and compassion. He saw with the eye of Unity, and continually encouraged others to do the same.

The selections gathered here might be used as daily reflections, each as a doorway to deeper connection with the Divine. We offer you these "jewels of remembrance" that you might hold them and catch the dancing Light reflected through them. May we be fed by that Light of Love and Unity and drawn ever closer into its bright center.

Listen, open a window to God
and begin to delight yourself
by gazing upon Him through the opening.
The business of love is to make that window in the heart,
for the breast is illumined by the beauty of the Beloved.
Gaze incessantly on the face of the Beloved!
Listen, this is in your power, my friend!

[VI, 3095-3097]

Camille Adams Helminski
Ramadan 1996, Putney, Vermont

Introduction

Under the Light of Mevlâna

"Nothing had prepared me for Rumi's words," someone said to me not long ago, "Not all my years of reading and writing poetry. Nor my years of spiritual searching." Many people know that experience, including those who had little interest in so-called "poetry." We are encountering more than a literary figure here in Mevlâna Jalâluddin Rumi, more than a poet. "Beware of the poets," the Qur'an says, "for they wander distractedly through the valleys, and *do not do what they say*." Mevlâna was all that he said; his words flowed like a fountain from his being. He had no literary ambition; he could not do otherwise than he did, and his prolific inspiration quenched the thirst of many hearts for the last seven centuries. As time passes his gift to humanity is recognized by more and more people.

There is no literary figure in Western culture to compare with him. Recently when an international conference was held to find a bridge between "Islam and the Occident," Mevlâna and Goethe were honored, but not even the Westerners attending felt that the two were of similar stature. "As great as Goethe is," Annemarie Schimmel, the great German scholar of Islam, remarked, "he is like a piece of the earth, while Mevlâna. . . Mevlâna is the whole sky." And Shakespeare, despite his greatness, is not alive in the hearts of people today as Mevlâna is. No, if we were to offer any cultural figure who is both timeless and sublime and whose influence seems never to diminish, it might be Bach.

Mevlâna's gift is "a lamp in the darkness of imagination, confusion, fantasy, doubt, and suspicion."[2] His masterwork, the *Mathnâwi*, consisting of six books and approximately 27,500 couplets, consists of interwoven stories, metaphysical reflections, and flights of lyric inspiration. No department of life escapes the light of this lamp; nothing is too profane or insignificant. Every imaginable subject and theme serves to reveal the master truth of reality: that all of life is one, that everything comes from God and returns to God, that behind all appearances a divine intention is being fulfilled, and that the purpose of all of this is to allow the reality of Love to be discovered and more completely known.

Every shop has a different kind of merchandise:
the Mathnawi is the shop for spiritual poverty, my son.
In the shoemaker's shop there is fine leather:
if you see wood there it is only the mold for a shoe.
The drapers have silk and dun-colored cloth in their shops:
if iron is there, it is only to serve as a yard-stick.
Our Mathnawi is the shop for Unity:
anything you see there other than the One God
is just an idol.

[*Mathnâwi* VI, 1525-1528]

Mevlâna is telling us: do not be distracted by all these characters and stories; everything I am saying means one thing. The "poverty" Mevlâna is referring to is an ontological poverty, the need of this whole material existence for God. All of "existence" is as nothing compared to the Divine Reality which is the Source of every thing, every action, every

[2]From the opening of Book Six of the *Mathnâwi*.

quality. The workshop of poverty is this material existence where everything is the manifestation of that One Divine Being which alone truly has Being. In relation to this Being we are only the borrowers of qualities. This, at least, is the negative statement of that Truth. To state it positively: all existences and all levels of existence are held within a loving and generous Unity.

The truth and the vision of Mevlâna is neither unique nor unprecendented within the tradition of Sufism. What is unique is the extent and completeness of his elaboration of this vision. No other human being who has worked in the medium of human language has so lucidly and beautifully expressed not only the human experience, but life itself in its completeness. He expresses the truth not only of humans, but of all the kingdoms of nature, as well as less tangible realms of existence. Most importantly, he reveals what it means to be a complete human being.

Now here is an expression that deserves our attention: *a Complete Human Being*. This is the essential contribution of Islamic Sufism to the human community. The Complete Human Being, *al-Insan al-Kamil*, is complete by virtue of having attained to all the levels of reality that are possible for a human. The Complete Human Being has realized within his or her own being all the attributes of the divine and has harmonized the individual will and intelligence with the divine will and intelligence.

The saint's greeting of peace has become God's greeting,
because the saint has set fire to the household of self.
He or she has died to self
and become living through the Sustainer,
so the mysteries of God flow from the lips.
The death of the body in self-discipline is life:
the sufferings of the body

are the cause of everlastingness to the spirit.

[*Mathnâwi* III, 3363-5]

While the Complete Human may be the rarest achievment of nature, such a person is the most human of human beings and shows through his or her own self the direction in which all of us must travel if we are to fulfill our human nature. From the Sufi point of view, the saint, the intimate of God, has not divorced or transcended life but has integrated the truth of the higher worlds into this world, and thereby brought light into the darkness of this material existence. With this light what was obscure becomes more clear, what appeared meaningless is revealed as purposeful. With this light fear becomes hope, doubt becomes trust, and preoccupation with the self becomes the unconditional love of every manifestation of life. The Complete Human Being has learned to live from the Heart, from the Divine Center.

The Real Way of the Heart

The Sufis understand the human Heart to be the macrocosm, not just the microcosm of the universe. While in outward form a human being is the microcosm, a miniature universe, in truth—according to the masters and prophets—mankind is the macrocosm, the cause of the existing universe.

This subject is being debated today in cosmological physics. It appears to those who have done the necessary calculations on the formation of the universe, that if you were to change any one of the physical laws one iota, there would neither be a universe that could support the human being, nor would there be a universe at all. It appears to those who have looked carefully that the universe was virtually designed to create the human being.

Maybe this is what Mevlâna Jalâluddin Rumi means when he says that the fruit is the cause of the tree. In the simplest terms, the Gardener planted the tree in order for it to bear fruit. How many fruit are on a tree? How many trees are within the fruit?

In the Islamic tradition God says: "I created the whole universe for you and you for Myself."[3] It is also said, "The heavens and the earth cannot contain Me; only the heart of My faithful servant is expansive enough to contain Me." The heart is not merely the seat of emotion; it is a potentially infinite inner space in which the Divine Reality can abide.

Entering Mevlâna's Universe of Love

The modernist dogma has it that this is an impersonal material universe, a universe which is more darkness than light, more cold than warmth, more vacuum than substance. Furthermore, many people feel that the random, isolated consciousness at the heart of each human life is threatened by vast forces that do not recognize its fragile existence.

For those with spiritual vision, however, we are living *within* an infinite ocean of Spirit. This whole universe is a manifestation of cosmic love.

Day and night there is movement of foam on the Sea.
You see the foam, but not the Sea. Amazing!
We are dashing against each other like boats:
our eyes are darkened though we are in clear water.
O you who have gone to sleep in the body's boat,
you've seen the water,
but look at the Water of the water.
The water has a Water that is driving it;
the spirit has a Spirit that is calling it.

[*Mathnâwi* III 1272-1274]

[3]Hadith Qudsi (An extra-Qur'anic revelation transmitted by Muhammad)

This universe is an expression of love. We live in an ocean of Love, but because it is so near to us, we need to look beyond appearances, beyond our preconceptions, and sometimes we need to be shocked, hurt, or experience some loss in order to be aware of the nearness and importance of love. Every being and thing in creation is set in motion by love. The planets revolve around the sun, and the sun radiates its energy to the planets. Atoms are held in a delicate but immensely powerful balance by love. Every species has its own form of love or desire which motivates it. Every human being has its own unique form of love through which it approaches life. Everything is seeking union with the object of its desire. And all of these desires are the derivatives of one Love. Love is the motivation behind every yearning.

Love is seeking to discover itself. This describes what is happening in all of life. We come into this world, and we experience a profound forgetfulness; we are asleep. Everything that happens from then on is the process of waking up to the fact that Love brought us here, that we are loved by a Beneficent Unseen Reality, and that the core of our being is Love. The whole purpose and meaning of creation is to discover the secret of Love.

You know the value of every article of merchandise,
but if you don't know the value of your own soul,
it's all foolishness.
You've come to know the fortunate and the inauspicious stars;
but you don't know whether you yourself
are fortunate or unlucky.
This, this is the essence of all sciences—
that you should know who you will be
when the Day of Reckoning arrives.

[*Mathnâwi* III 2652-2654]

Love is both mystery and knowledge. Furthermore, it is a mystery that has spoken to us about Itself in the form of those revelations that have profoundly altered the course and quality of human history. The lives and teachings of Buddha, Jesus, and Muhammad, among others, have influenced and transformed so many billions of people because they are essentially teachings of love.

The experience of love is the most fulfilling and important experience we can have, the highest of all values. We can't compare love to anything. It is its own meaning and its own criteria. Since everything is explained by something subtler than what is being explained, nothing can explain love because love itself is the subtlest of all things we can experience.

Love is seeking us. Love brought us here, whether we know it or not. Love nudges us to make plans, to seek relationship, to create the possibility of a meeting of hearts. It puts the pen to paper; it puts a word on the tongue. Love is not the goal of anything; it is the cause of everything.

See how the hand is invisible while the pen is writing;
the horse careening, yet the rider is unseen;
the arrow flying, but the bow out of sight;
individual souls existing,
while the Soul of souls is hidden.

[*Mathnâwi* II,1303-1304]

The spiritual life requires a reversal of our usual egoistic thinking and wanting. We believe that we are seeking, but what if it is Love itself that is the seeker? Rumi says, "Abundance is seeking the beggars and the poor, just as beauty seeks a mirror. . . . Beggars, then, are the mirrors of

God's abundance, and they who are with God are united with absolute abundance."[4]

The Sufis know that Love is the most active, the most powerful force in the universe. We think we are the creators and directors of our lives, but our actions may be just the slightest visible signs of a process that is vast and invisible. Love is always acting on us. We know only a fragment of what can be seen; what is of the unseen we know very little. We are unconscious of all the forces and factors that sustain us, care for us, that guide our life and our world, and that bring our incipient humanness to its completion. Mevlâna's message is to surrender ourselves to the creative power of this Love and to consciously make a call:

O You who make demands within me like an embryo,
since You are the one who makes the demand,
make its fulfillment easy;
show the way, help me,
or else relinquish Your claim
and take this burden from me!
Since from a debtor You're demanding gold,
give him gold in secret, O rich King!

[*Mathnâwi* III 1490-1492]

The idea that we live in Love's Universe may seem a sentimental and naive proposition to some people. Why then do we live in a world of such injustices and horrors? Life brings us very real suffering, and this suffering can be the cause of some doubt about the beneficence of life. Often when we are in the midst of our suffering we cannot see a purpose in it. We may lose our trust in the meaning of life. The soul faces a critical choice at this point: whether to be embittered by certain experiences or to allow the pain of life

---

[4] *Mathnâwi* I, 2745, 2750.

to reorient us to a deeper truth, to help us form a connection to a reality beyond space, time, and even beyond our individual selves.

In time We shall make them fully understand Our signs
in the farthest horizons and within themselves,
so that it will become clear to them
that this [revelation] is indeed the truth.
Is it not enough to know that your Sustainer
is a witness to everything?

[Qur'an: Surah 41:53]

The idea that we live in a universe created by love is anything but sentimental and naive, if we do not deny the pain of life but embrace this complex reality with all its contradictions. We see that we are turned from one feeling to another and taught by means of opposites and contrasts.

He alone has the right to break,
for He alone has the power to mend.
He that knows how to sew together
knows how to tear apart:
whatever He sells,
He buys something better in exchange.
He lays the house in ruins;
then in a moment He makes it more liveable than before.

[*Mathnâwi* I, 3882]

Sometimes we need to be shocked out of our complacency and indifference to know the reality of love. We need to find a way to restore the proper perspective. We need to be reminded of the centrality of Love. We begin to see the infinite power of Love as the greatest cause in the universe and little by little we begin to serve it. Without becoming passive, we stop resisting and surrender. Eventually, we begin to see the truth of the Sufi notion that even a bitter drink is sweet when it is from the Beloved. Knowing that Love is the master of the universe helps us to accept and learn from every experience. Knowing that there is an eternal dimension residing here in intimate association with material existence will begin to free us from fears. When we are less governed by negative thoughts about reality, we will be freed from many fears.

The seven heavens extol God's limitless glory,
and the earth, and all that they contain;
and there is not a single thing
that does not acclaim God's limitless glory and praise,
but you [O human beings] fail to grasp
the manner of their glorification of the One
who is truly forbearing, and very forgiving!

[Qur'an: Surah 17: 44]

This is the merciful and beneficent reality that Mevlâna saw reflected in every aspect of existence. Inscribed above Rumi's tomb in Konya, Turkey are these words which sum up the accomplishment of Mevlâna in the words of one of his own contemporaries, Sadreddin Konevi, the great interpreter of Ibn 'Arabi:

In the name of God, the merciful and compassionate. We can only call on Him for help. A good end awaits those who commit no sins. God has no enemies but the cruel and unjust. He who visits the world of sleep and rest is sacred. Here is the resting place of Mevlâna, sultan of the wise, shining light of God illuminating the darkness, an imam and son of an imam, support of Islam, a guide leading people into God's glorious presence, who expounds the miracles long after their evidence has disappeared, who enlightens the nearest ways after the signs which once showed them were lost, who is the key to the treasures of heaven, who explains the treasures of the earth, who decorates the gardens of the hearts of people with flowers of truth, the light of the eye of perfection, the soul of grace, who embellishes the necks of the world's people of wisdom with necklaces of love, who distinguishes the true from the false, the pole of God's scholars who penetrated the mysteries of the Qur'an.

★ ★ ★

And so we have revealed a life-giving message to you,
coming from Us.
Before this you did not know what revelation is,
nor what faith implies;
but now we have caused this message to be a light,
by which We guide those of Our servants whom we will,
and truly you shall guide people to the straight way as well.

[Qur'an: Surah 42: 52.]

Kabir Helminski
Ramadan 1996, Putney, Vermont

A Note on Translation

A translator must ask the question: What is it that I am translating? Words? Ideas? Poetry? Spirit? And what is the purpose of my translation? Of those selections which seem to epitomize Mevlâna's understanding and vision, we have chosen those that lend themselves to translation, which somehow open up possibilities within our own language. We have then tried to allow language itself to do the work. If we have taken liberties, they have been mostly in non-essential areas: more gender-neutral language, and in some cases more explicit translation of obscure word-play. Although we have studied the Persian language, our work is to an extent based on Nicholson's somewhat literal rendering of the *Mathnâwi*, supported by more than twenty years of practice and study within the Mevlevi Sufi tradition itself. The meanings, after all, are not approachable through the words alone; some experience of the state and intention behind the words is necessary. Part of the training of this path is to allow one's self to become more transparent in order that something beyond oneself may come through. We pray that some transparency is offered here.

Dedicated to Dr. Celaleddin Celebi,
twenty-first generation grandson
of Mevlâna Jalâluddin Rumi

May God have mercy on those who lead the way
and those who come behind, and those who fulfill their vows,
and those who seek to fulfill them,
with His Grace and bounty, His great benefits and favors!
For He is the best object of petition and the noblest object of hope;
and God is the best protector and the most merciful
of those who show mercy,[5]
and the best of friends and the best of heirs
and the best replacer of what has been consumed
and provider for those devoted
who sow and till the soil of good works.
And God bless Muhammad and all the Prophets and Messengers!
Amen, O Lord of created beings!

[*Mathnâwi* IV, Prologue]

[5] Qur'an: Surah Yusuf (Joseph), 12:64.

Mouthfuls of food are the gift of every tree bearing fruit,
but the gift of a throat is from God alone.
He bestows a throat on the body and the spirit;
He gives an appropriate throat to every part of you.

[III, 17-18]

Where is the nurse for the thirsty infant
who with kindness would offer the taste of inner sweetness?
Where is she who would bar the way to her self
in order to open the way to a hundred gardens of delight?
For the breast has become a barrier between the infant
and other delicious tastes and countless nourishments.
Our life depends on weaning.
Strive to wean yourself little by little.
Wean yourself from this world's food
and become a healing sage like Luqman.[6]
Become a hunter of the hidden game.

[III, 46-49; 52]

---

[6] A Prophet mentioned in the Qur'an and known for his healing gifts.

Don't strive so much to complete your worldly affairs;
don't strive in any affair that's not sacred.

Otherwise at the end, you'll leave incomplete,
your spiritual affairs damaged and your bread unbaked.

The beautifying of your grave isn't done
by means of wood and stone and plaster;

no, but by digging your grave in spiritual purity
and burying your own selfhood in His,

and by becoming His dust, buried in love of Him,
so that from His breath, yours may be replenished.

[III, 128-132]

The smell of pride and greed and lust
will betray you when you speak
as much as the onions you have eaten.
Many prayers are rejected because of their smell;
the corrupt heart reveals itself in the tongue.
But if your meaning is pure,
God will welcome even your clumsy expression.

[III, 166-171]

How many victories are won
without spiritual struggle and patience?
To show patience for the sake of the cup of Divine Knowledge
is no hardship:
show patience, for patience is the key to joy.

[III, 211-212]

Although he was a mountain,
relying only upon his own firmness,
a small flood swept him away.

When the Decree extends its head from heaven,
the intelligent become deaf and blind;
fish are cast from the sea;
birds are miserably caught in the snare.

All are lost except
the one who takes refuge
within the command of God:
no unfortunate aspect among the stars
was ever the cause of shed blood.

Unless you take refuge with the Decree,
nothing you can devise
will ever gain your freedom.

[III, 468-470; 472-473]

Reap the benefit of God's beneficence in these words:
"For my Sustainer does not love excessive rejoicing."
Rein in your joy for all He causes to come to you,
for the gifts that preoccupy you
divert you from Him.
Rejoice in Him, rejoice in nothing but Him.

[III, 505-507]

If anybody goes traveling without a guide,
every two days' journey
becomes a journey of a hundred years.
The one who takes up a profession
without having had a teacher
becomes a laughing-stock,
no matter where he lives.
Except perhaps for a single occurrence,
in all the world, is a descendant of Adam
ever born without parents?
The one who earns gains wealth;
it's a rare event
to find a buried treasure.

[III, 588; 590-592]

There are hundreds of thousands of trials for anyone who claims,
"I am the commander of the gate."
If the vulgar don't put him to the test,
the adepts of the way will demand the token of his sincerity.
When a roughneck pretends to be a tailor,
the king will throw down a piece of satin in front of him.

[III, 682-684]

Both the dry and the fresh branch are near to the sun;
how can the sun be screened off from either?
But how much greater is the nearness of the bough
from which you enjoy ripe fruit?
From its nearness to the sun,
let the dry branch, if it can,
get anything besides withering sooner!
O man without wisdom,
don't be the kind of drunkard
who returns to his wits a sorry man.
Be one of those who drink the wine of Love,
and whose drunkenness mature intellects long for.

[III, 707-711]

You sweeten your palate with the savor of fantasy;
you blow into the bag of selfhood and fill it up.
Then, one prick of the needle and you are emptied of air.
May no intelligent man be so full of wind!

[III, 718-719]

Vain, boastful talk repels acts of kindness
and tears the branch of mercy from the trunk of the tree.
Speak honestly or else be silent,
and then behold grace and delight in it.

[III, 751-752]

Because Pharaoh's toil was not blessed by God,
whatever he would stitch,
that stitching was in effect a ripping apart.

[III, 840]

Whether one moves slowly or with speed,
the one who is a seeker will be a finder.
Always seek with your whole self,
for the search is an excellent guide on the way.
Though you are lame and limping,
though your figure is bent and clumsy,
always creep towards the One. Make that One your quest.
By speech and by silence and by fragrance,
catch the scent of the King everywhere.

[III, 978-981]

With us, one needs to be a waking sleeper,
that in the state of wakefulness,
you may dream dreams.
The thought of created things
is an enemy to this sweet waking sleep;
until your thought is asleep, your throat is shut,
no mysteries can enter.
Mystical bewilderment must sweep thought away;
bewilderment devours thought
and recollection of anything other than God.

[III, 1114-1116]

The most secure place to hide a treasure of gold
is in some desolate, unnoticed place.
Why would anyone hide treasure
in plain sight?
And so it is said,
"Joy is hidden beneath sorrow."

[III, 1133-1134]

There is many a one whose eye is awake
but whose heart is asleep.
What, in truth, should be seen
by the eyes of creatures of water and clay?
The one who keeps her heart awake,
though the eye of her head may sleep,
her heart will open a hundred eyes.

[III, 1222-1223]

Day and night there is movement of foam on the Sea.
You see the foam, but not the Sea. Amazing!
We are dashing against each other like boats:
our eyes are darkened though we're in clear water.
O you who've gone to sleep in the body's boat,
you've seen the water,
but look at the Water of the water.
The water has a Water that is driving it;
the spirit has a Spirit that is calling it.

[III, 1271-1274]

This world is like a tree,
and we are the half-ripe fruit upon it.
Unripe fruit clings tight to the branch
because, immature, it's not ready for the palace.
When fruits become ripe, sweet and juicy,
then biting their lips, they loosen their hold.
When the mouth has been sweetened by felicity,
the kingdom of the world loses its appeal.
To be tightly attached to the world signifies immaturity;
as long as you're an embryo,
blood-drinking is your business.

[III, 1293-1297]

When you fall asleep,
you go from the presence of yourself
into your own true presence.
You hear something
and surmise that someone else in your dream
has secretly informed you.
You are not a single "you."
No, you are the sky and the deep sea.
Your mighty "Thou," which is nine hundredfold,
is the ocean, the drowning place
of a hundred "thou's" within you.

[III, 1300-1303]

Noah said, "I don't look at anyone but You;
even if I do, it's only a pretext,
for You are the real object of my glance.
I am in love with Your making—
both in the moment of thankfulness,
and when patience is required.
How should I be in love, like the unfaithful,
with that which You have made?"
The one who loves God's making is glorious;
the one who loves what God has made has no faith.

[III, 1359-1361]

When the kernel swells the walnut shell,
or the pistachio, or the almond, the husk diminishes.
As the kernel of knowledge grows,
the husk thins and disappears,
because the lover is consumed by the beloved.
Since the quality of being sought is the opposite of seeking,
revelation and divine lightning
consume the prophet with fire.
When the attributes of the Eternal shine forth,
the cloak of temporality is burned away.

[III, 1388-1391]

"I am only the house of your beloved,
not the beloved herself:
true love is for the treasure,
not for the coffer that contains it."
The real beloved is that one who is unique,
who is your beginning and your end.
When you find that one,
you'll no longer expect anything else:
that one is both the manifest and the mystery.
That one is the lord of states of feeling,
dependent on none:
month and year are slaves to that moon.
When He bids the "state,"
it does His bidding;
when that one wills, bodies become spirit.

[III, 1417-1421]

Even though you're not equipped,
keep searching:
equipment isn't necessary on the way to the Lord.
Whoever you see engaged in search,
become her friend and cast your head in front of her,
for choosing to be a neighbor of seekers,
you become one yourself;
protected by conquerors,
you will yourself learn to conquer.
If an ant seeks the rank of Solomon,
don't smile contemptuously upon its quest.
Everything you possess of skill, and wealth and handicraft,
wasn't it first merely a thought and a quest?

[III, 1445-1449]

O You who make demands within me like an embryo,
since You are the one who makes the demand,
make its fulfillment easy;
show the way, help me,
or else relinquish Your claim
and take this burden from me!
Since from a debtor You're demanding gold,
give him gold in secret, O rich King!

[III, 1490-1492]

Everyone can distinguish mercy from wrath,
whether he is wise or ignorant or corrupt,
but a mercy hidden in wrath,
or wrath hidden in the heart of mercy
can only be recognized by one whose heart
contains a spiritual touchstone.

[III, 1506-1508]

Each creature glorifies You in a different way,
and each is unaware of the states of the other.
The human being doesn't believe that stones utter praise,
but inanimate things are masters of worship.
The seventy-two sects are dubious about each other's state.
Since I pay no attention to the glorification of one who speaks,
how should my heart recognize
the worship offered by the mute?

[III, 1496-1498; 1500]

When a man is busy in earnest,
he is unconscious of his pain.
I mention this insensibility to pain
so you may know how much the body resembles a garment.
Go, seek the one who wears it;
don't kiss a piece of cloth.

[III, 1610]

Just as staying home is easy for some,
traveling comes easily to others.
Each of us was made for some particular work,
and the desire for that work has been placed in our hearts.
How should hand and foot be set in motion without desire?
If you see your desire leading toward Heaven,
unfold your wings to claim it;
but if you see your desire bends to the earth,
keep lamenting.
The wise weep in the beginning;
the foolish beat their heads at the end.
Discern the end from the beginning
so that you may not be repenting
when the Day of Reckoning arrives.

[III, 1616-1623]

This world is a dream—don't be deluded;
if in a dream a hand is lost, it's no harm.
In dreams, no real damage is done
if the body is maimed or torn in two hundred pieces.
The Prophet said of this apparently substantial world
that it is but the sleeper's dream.
You've accepted this as an idea,
but the spiritual traveler has beheld this truth with open eye.
You are asleep in the daytime; don't say this is not sleep.

[III, 1729; 1732-1735]

Sense perception is captive to the intellect;
know also that intellect is captive to spirit.
The spirit sets free the shackled hand of intellect
and brings its embarrassed affairs into harmony.

[III, 1824-1825]

The one who is ruled by mind,
without sleeping, puts her senses to sleep,
so that unseen things may emerge from the world of the soul.
Even in her waking state, she dreams dreams,
and opens thereby the gates of Heaven.

[III, 1833-1834]

The bird, patience, flies faster than all the others.
What is easy will be made difficult by your impatience.

[III, 1847]

Wherever the Eternal Command takes its course,
living and dying are one to God's willing servant.
He lives for God's sake, not for riches;
he dies for God's sake, not from fear and pain.
His faith exists for the sake of doing God's will,
not for the sake of Paradise and its trees and streams.
His abandonment of infidelity is also for God's sake,
and not out of fear of the Fire.

[III, 1909-1912]

By God, don't linger
in any spiritual benefit you have gained,
but yearn for more—like one suffering from illness
whose thirst for water is never quenched.
This Divine Court is the Plane of the Infinite.
Leave the seat of honor behind;
let the Way be your seat of honor.

[III, 1960-1961]

Hours make the young old.
All changes have arisen from the hours:
the one who is freed from hours is freed from change.
When for an hour you escape from the hours,
"how" no longer remains:
you become familiar with that which is without "how."
Hours are not acquainted with timelessness.
For the one who is possessed by time,
there is no way there except bewilderment.

[III, 2073-2076]

God accepts the utmost exertion of one who has little to give.
God accepts a crust of bread and absolves the giver;
from the eyes of a blind man, two drops of light are enough.

[III, 2115-2117]

Since the object of praise is one,
from this point of view,
all religions are but one religion.
Know that all praise belongs to the Light of God
and is only lent to created forms and beings.
Should people praise anyone but the One
who alone deserves to be praised?
But they go astray in useless fantasy.
The Light of God in relation to phenomena
is like a light shining upon a wall—
the wall is but a focus for these splendors.

[III, 2124-2127]

People are distracted by objects of desire,
and afterwards repent of the lust they've indulged,
because they have indulged with a phantom
and are left even farther from Reality than before.
Your desire for the illusory is a wing,
by means of which a seeker might ascend to Reality.
When you have indulged a lust, your wing drops off;
you become lame and that fantasy flees.
Preserve the wing and don't indulge such lust,
so that the wing of desire may bear you to Paradise.
People fancy they are enjoying themselves,
but they are really tearing out their wings
for the sake of an illusion.

[III, 2133-2138]

On Resurrection Day God will ask,
"During this reprieve I gave you,
what have you produced for Me?
Through what work have you reached your life's end?
Your food and your strength, for what have they been consumed?
Where have you dimmed the luster of your eye?
Where have you dissipated your five senses?
You have expended eyes and ears and intellect
and the pure celestial substances;
what have you purchased from the earth?
I gave you hands and feet as spade and mattock
for tilling the soil of good works;
when did they by themselves become existent?"

[III, 2149-2153]

From the ritual prayer, which is as the egg,
hatches the chick;
don't peck like a bird
without reverence or felicity.

[III, 2175]

The lion of destiny is dragging our souls,
preoccupied with the business of the world,
into the jungles of death.
People fear poverty,
plunged as they are up to their necks in briny water.
If they feared the Creator of poverty,
treasures would reveal themselves.
Through fear of affliction,
they sink into the very essence of affliction:
in their quest for life in the world,
they have lost it.

[III, 2204-2207]

O heart, you will be regarded with favor by God
at the moment when, like a part, you move towards your Whole.

[III, 2243]

Come, seek, for search is the foundation of fortune:
every success depends upon focusing the heart.
Unconcerned with the business of the world,
keep saying with all your soul, "Coo, Coo," like the dove.
Consider this well, O you whom worldliness veils:
God has linked our invocation to the promise, "I will answer."
When weakness is cleared from your heart,
your prayer will reach the glorious Lord.

[III, 2302-2305]

During prayer I am accustomed to turn to God like this
and recall the meaning of the words of the Tradition,
"the delight felt in the ritual prayer."[7]
The window of my soul opens,
and from the purity of the unseen world,
the book of God comes to me straight.
The book, the rain of divine grace, and the light
are falling into my house through a window
from my real and original source.
The house without a window is hell;
to make a window is the essence of true religion.
Don't thrust your ax upon every thicket;
come, use your ax to cut open a window.

[III, 2401-2405]

[7] The Prophet Muhammad (peace and blessings be upon him) is said to have mentioned this as one of the three things he loved best in the world.

The philosopher is a slave of intellectual perceptions;
the pure saint rides the Intellect of intellects like a prince.
The Intellect of intellect is your kernel;
the intellect is only the husk.
The belly of animals keeps seeking husks.
The intellect blackens books with writing;
the Intellect of intellect fills the universe
with light from the moon of reality.
It is free from blackness or whiteness:
the light of its moon rises and shines
upon the heart and the soul.

[III, 2527-2528; 2531-2532]

The Logos is digging a channel
for water to reach the next generation.
During every generation there is one who brings the word of God;
still the sayings of those who have come before are helpful.

[III, 2537-2538]

Flee from the foolish; even Jesus fled from them.
Much blood has been shed by companionship with fools!
Air absorbs water little by little;
even so, the fool drains you of spirit.
He steals your heat and leaves you cold,
like one who puts a stone beneath you.
The flight of Jesus wasn't caused by fear,
for he is safe from the mischief of fools;
his purpose was to teach by example.

[III, 2595-2598]

Children tell stories,
but in their tales are enfolded
many a mystery and moral lesson.
Though they may relate many ridiculous things,
keep looking in those ruined places for a treasure.

[III, 2602-2603]

Hope is the deaf man who has often heard of our dying,
but hasn't heard of his own death or contemplated his own end.
The blind man is Greed: he sees the faults of others,
hair by hair, and broadcasts them from street to street,
but of his own faults his blind eyes perceive nothing.
The naked man fears his cloak will be pulled off,
but how could anyone take the cloak of one who is naked?
The worldly man is destitute and terrified:
he possesses nothing, yet he dreads thieves.
Bare he came and naked he goes,
yet all the while he's agonizing about thieves.
When death comes, everyone around him is lamenting,
while his own spirit begins to laugh at his fear.
At that moment the rich man knows he has no gold,
and the keen-witted man sees that talent does not belong to him.

[III, 2628-2635]

You know the value of every article of merchandise,
but if you don't know the value of your own soul,
it's all foolishness.
You've come to know the fortunate and the inauspicious stars,
but you don't know whether you yourself
are fortunate or unlucky.
This, this is the essence of all sciences—
that you should know who you will be
when the Day of Reckoning arrives.

[III, 2652-2654]

The fowler scatters grain incessantly:
the grain is visible, but the deceit is hidden.
Wherever you see the grain, beware,
lest the trap confine your wings.
The bird that gives up that grain
eats from Reality's spacious field.
With that it is content and escapes;
no trap confines its feathers.
Many times have you fallen into the snare of greed
and given your throat up to be cut;
but again the One that disposes hearts to repentance
has set you free, accepted your repentance,
and made you rejoice.
O moth, don't be forgetful and dubious;
just look at your burnt wing.

[III, 2858-2861; 2870-2871; 2879]

Giving thanks for abundance
is sweeter than the abundance itself:
Should one who is absorbed with the Generous One
be distracted by the gift?
Thankfulness is the soul of beneficence;
abundance is but the husk,
for thankfulness brings you to the place where the Beloved lives.
Abundance yields heedlessness;
thankfulness, alertness:
hunt for bounty with the snare of gratitude to the King.

[III, 2895-2897]

I did not create the Jinn and mankind
except that they might worship Me.[8]
Recite this text.
The final object of this world is nothing but divine worship.
Though the final object of a book is the science which it contains,
you can also make it a pillow to rest upon;
it will serve as that, too.
But being a pillow was not its real aim.
It was really intended for learning and knowledge
and the benefit that comes from these.

[III, 2988-2990]

---

[8] Qur'an: Surah Adh-Dhariyat (The Dust-Scattering Winds), 51:56.

The lover's food is the love of the bread;
no bread need be at hand:
no one who is sincere in his love is a slave to existence.
Lovers have nothing to do with existence;
lovers have the interest without the capital.
Without wings they fly around the world;
without hands they carry off the polo ball from the field.
That dervish who caught the scent of Reality
used to weave baskets even though his hands had been cut off.
Lovers have pitched their tents in non-existence:
they are of one quality and one essence, as non-existence is.

[III, 3020-3024]

Many learned men gain no profit from their knowledge:
those who commit knowledge to memory,
but are not in love with it.

[III, 3038]

The sea doesn't let the fish out,
nor does it let the creatures of the earth in.
Water is the original home of the fish;
the weighty animal is of the earth.
Nothing we can do can change this.
The lock of Divine destiny is strong,
and the only opener is God:
cling to surrender and contentment with God's will.
Though the atoms, one by one, should become keys,
yet this opening is not effected except by divine Majesty.
When you forget your own scheming,
happiness will come to you from your spiritual guide.
When you are forgetful of self,
you are remembered by God;
when you have become God's slave,
then you are set free.

[III, 3071-3076]

When it comes to earning food,
why has the fear of eternal disappointment
not waylaid you?
You'll say, "Though I face the fear of disappointment,
fear increases when I'm idle.
My hope increases when I work;
when I'm idle, I risk more."
Why does the fear of loss
restrain you when it comes to faith?
Haven't you seen how gainfully employed
the prophets and saints are?
Haven't you seen what mines of treasure
have opened to them
from frequenting the shop of Spirit?

[III, 3096-3101]

The power of free action is your profit earning capital.
Pay attention!
Watch over the moment of power and observe it well!
The human being rides on the steed of
We have honored the children of Adam.[9]
The reins of free-will are in the hand of intelligence.

[III, 3299-3300]

---

[9] Qur'an: Al-Isra (The Night Journey), 17:70.

It was Mary's painful need that made the infant Jesus
begin to speak from the cradle.
Whatever grew has grown for the sake of those in need,
so that a seeker might find the thing he sought.
If God most High has created the heavens,
He has created them for the purpose of satisfying needs.
Wherever a pain is, that's where the cure goes;
wherever poverty is, that's where provision goes.
Wherever a difficult question is,
that's where the answer goes;
wherever a ship is, water goes to it.
Don't seek the water; increase your thirst,
so water may gush forth from above and below.
Until the tender-throated babe is born,
how should the milk for it
flow from the mother's breast?

[III, 3204; 3208-3213]

Whatever by divine destiny becomes lost to you,
know for sure it has saved you from difficulty.
Some one once asked, "What is Sufism?"
The Shaikh replied,
"To feel joy in the heart at the coming of sorrow."
Regard His chastisement as the eagle
which carried off the Prophet's boot,
that she might save his foot from the serpent's bite.
O happy is the understanding that is not dusty and dim.
God has said, *Grieve not for that which escapes you,*[10]
if the wolf comes and destroys your sheep,
for that God-sent affliction keeps away greater afflictions,
and that loss prevents much greater losses.

[III, 3260-3265]

The intelligent person sees with the heart
the result from the beginning;
the one lacking in knowledge
only discovers it at the end.

[III, 3372]

[10] Qur'an: Surah Al-Hadid (Iron), 57:23.

To learn the secret of the Unseen
is only fitting for that one
who can seal her lips and keep silent.

[III, 3387]

The core of every fruit is better than its rind:
consider the body to be the rind,
and its friend the spirit to be the core.
After all, the Human Being has a goodly core;
seek it for one moment
if you are of those inspired by the Divine breath.

[III, 3417-8]

Everyone's death is of the same quality as himself, my lad:
to the enemy of God, an enemy; to the friend of God, a friend.
Your fear of death in fleeing from it
is really your fear of yourself.
Pay attention, O dear soul!

[III, 3439; 3441]

God brought the earth and heavenly spheres into existence
through the deliberation of six days—
even though He was able through "*Be, and it is*"[11]
to bring forth a hundred earths and heavens.
Little by little until forty years of age
that Sovereign raises the human being to completion,
although in a single moment He was able
to send fifty flying up from non-existence.
Jesus by means of one prayer could make the dead spring to life:
is the Creator of Jesus unable
to suddenly bring full-grown human beings
fold by fold into existence?
This deliberation is for the purpose of teaching you
that you must seek God slowly, without any break.
A little stream which moves continually
doesn't become tainted or foul.
From this deliberation are born felicity and joy:
this deliberation is the egg;
good fortune is the bird that comes forth.

[III, 3500-3508]

[11] Qur'an: Surah Ya Sin (O Thou Human Being), 36:82.

The world is a spell that blinds the eye:
it appears wide when in reality it's narrow.
It's laughter is weeping;
its glory is but shame.

[III, 3543-3544]

The body is a narrow house,
and the soul within is cramped.
God ruined it so that He might make a royal palace.
I am cramped like the embryo in the womb:
I 've become nine-months old.
This migration is now urgent,
but unless the throes of childbirth overtake my mother,
what am I to do?
In this prison I am amidst the fire.
My mother, my bodily nature,
with its death throes is birthing spirit,
so that the lamb may be released from the ewe,
and begin to graze in the green fields.
Come, open your womb, for this lamb has grown big.

[III, 3555-3559]

There is no dervish in the world;
and if there be a dervish, that dervish is really non-existent.
In essence he exists,
but his attributes are non-existent within God's.

[III, 3669-3670]

The penetrating intellect, when separated from its friends,
becomes like an archer whose bow is broken.
When something makes you rejoice in this world,
consider at that moment the parting from it.
Many have been gladdened by what made you glad,
yet in the end like the wind it escaped.
It will escape from you, too: don't set your heart upon it.
Escape from it before it flies from you.
Before the slipping away of your possessions,
say to the form of created things, like Mary,
"*I take refuge from you with the Merciful God.*"[12]

[III, 3693; 3698-3700]

---

[12] Qur'an: Surah Maryam (Mary), 19:18.

When a feeling of spiritual contraction comes over you,
O traveler, it's for your own good.
Don't burn with grief,
for in the state of expansion and delight you are spending.
That enthusiasm requires an income of pain to balance it.
If it were always summer,
the sun's blazing heat would burn the garden
to the roots and depths of the soil.
The withered plants never again would become fresh.
If December is sour-faced, yet it is kind.
Summer is laughing, but yet it destroys.
When spiritual contraction comes,
behold expansion within it;
be cheerful and let your face relax.

[III, 3734-3739]

Observe the qualities of expansion and contraction
in the fingers of your hand:
surely after the closing of the fist comes the opening.
If the fingers were always closed or always open,
the owner would be crippled.
Your movement is governed by these two qualities:
they are as necessary to you
as two wings are to a bird.

[III, 3762-3766]

A beloved said to her lover,
"O youth, you've visited many cities,
which of them is the fairest?"
He replied, "The city where my sweetheart is."
Wherever the carpet is spread for our King,
there is the spacious plain,
even though it be as narrow as the eye of a needle.
Wherever a Joseph radiant as the moon may be,
Paradise is there, even though it be the bottom of a well.

[III, 3808-3811]

For lovers, there is a dying in every moment:
truly, the dying of lovers is not of one kind.
The lover has been given two hundred lives
from the Soul of Guidance;
each instant she sacrifices another.
For each life she gives, she receives ten:
as it is said in the Qur'an "*ten like unto them.*"[13]
If my blood were shed by that friendly Face,
dancing triumphantly I would lavish my life upon Him.
I have tried it: this life is my death;
and when I escape from this life, it is to endure forever.
"Kill me, kill me, O trusty friends!
For in my being killed is life upon life."[14]
O You who make the cheek radiant,
O Spirit of everlastingness, draw my spirit to Yourself
and generously bestow upon me the meeting with You.

[III, 3834-3840]

[13] Qur'an: Surah Hud, 11:13.

[14] A quote from the martyr Al-Hallaj.

For lovers, the only lecturer is the beauty of the Beloved:
their only book and lecture and lesson is the Face.
Outwardly they are silent,
but their penetrating remembrance rises
to the high throne of their Friend.
Their only lesson is enthusiasm, whirling, and trembling,
not the precise points of law.

[III, 3847-3849]

O my noble friends, slaughter this cow,
if you wish to raise up the spirit of insight.
I died to being mineral and growth began.
I died to vegetable growth and attained to the state of animals.
I died from animality and became Adam:
why then should I fear?
When have I become less by dying?
Next I shall die to being a human being,
so that I may soar and lift up my head among the angels.
Yet I must escape even from that angelic state:
everything is perishing except His Face.[15]
Once again I shall be sacrificed, dying to the angelic;
I shall become that which could never be imagined —
I shall become non-existent.
Non-existence sings its clear melody,
Truly, unto Him shall we return![16]

[III, 3900-3906]

---

[15] Qur'an: Surah Al-Qasas (The Story), 28:88.
[16] Qur'an: Surah Fussilat (Clearly Spelled Out), 41:21.

I am amazed at the seeker of purity
who when it's time to be polished
complains of rough-handling.
Love is like a lawsuit:
to suffer harsh treatment is the evidence;
when you have no evidence, the lawsuit is lost.
Don't grieve when the Judge demands your evidence;
kiss the snake so that you may gain the treasure.
That harshness isn't towards you, O son,
but towards the harmful qualities within you.
When someone beats a rug,
the blows are not against the rug,
but against the dust in it.

[III, 4008-4012]

If your grasping ego had not waylaid you from within,
would bandits have any power to lay a hand upon you?
Because of this demanding jailor, desire,
the heart is captive to greed, desire, and harm.
Because of that inner jailor, you've become a crazed thief
even more susceptible to that jailer's power.
Pay attention to the wise counsel of the Prophet:
"Your worst enemy is between your two sides."[17]

[III, 4063-4066]

---

[17] *Hadith* of the Prophet Muhammad.

In the plain where this virulent poison grew,
there has also grown the antidote, my son.
The antidote says to you, "Seek protection from me,
for I am nearer than the poison to you."

[III, 4076-4077]

The goods of this world and this body are melting snow;
yet God buys them, for it is said *God has purchased.*[18]
You prefer the melting snow to God's offer.
Because you are dubious, you have no certainty.
There is this marvellous opinion in you
which won't fly to that garden of certainty.
Every opinion is really thirsting for conviction
and flapping its wings in pursuit.
When it attains knowledge, then the wing becomes a foot,
and its knowledge begins to scent that garden.
In the tested Way,
knowledge is inferior to certainty but above opinion.
Know that knowledge is a seeker of certainty,
and certainty is a seeker of vision and intuition.

[III, 4115-4121]

[18] Qur'an: Surah At-Tawbah (Repentance), 9:111.

That which God said to the rose,
and caused it to laugh in full-blown beauty,
He said to my heart,
and made it a hundred times more beautiful.

[III, 4129]

I am the lover of that One to whom every "that" belongs:
of even a single pearl of His
the bodyguard is Intellect and Spirit.
I do not boast, or if I boast, it only seems that way,
for I have no trouble quenching fire.
How should I steal when He is the keeper of the treasury?
How should I not be bold and resolute?
He is my support.

[III, 4136-4138]

Everyone baked by the divine Sun
will become rock solid:
without dread or shame,
his features fiery and veil-rending,
like the face of the peerless Sun.
Every prophet was hard-faced in this world,
and beat single-handed against the army of kings,
and did not turn his face from fear or pain,
but single and alone
dashed against a whole world.
The stone is hard-faced and bold-eyed,
unafraid of the bricks thrown by the world.
For the bricks were made strong in the kiln,
but the rock was hardened by a Godly art.

[III, 4139-4144]

Your anguish is seeking a way to attain to Me:
yesterday evening I heard your deep sighs.
And I am able, without any delay,
to give you access, to show you a way of passage,
to deliver you from this whirlpool of time,
that you might set your foot upon the treasure of union with Me;
but the sweetness and delights of the resting place
are in proportion to the pain of the journey.
Only then will you enjoy your native town and your kinsfolk,
when you have suffered the anguish of exile.

[III, 4154-4158]

Look at the chickpea in the pot,
how it leaps up when it feels the fire.
While boiling, it continually rises to the top
and cries, "Why are you setting the fire under me?
Since you bought me, why are you turning me upside down?"
The housewife keeps hitting it with the ladle.
"No!" she says, "boil nicely now,
and don't leap away from the one who makes the fire.
It's not because you are hateful to me that I boil you,
but so that you might gain flavor,
and become nutritious and mingle with essential spirit.
This affliction is not because you are despised.
When you were green and fresh,
you were drinking water in the garden:
that water-drinking was for the sake of this fire."

[III, 4159-4165]

When you read the Qur'an
don't only look at the exterior, my son:
the Devil considers Adam as nothing more than clay.
The external sense of the Qur'an is like a person's form:
while his features are visible, his spirit is hidden.
Someone's uncles look at him for a hundred years,
and yet of his inward state
don't see so much as the tip of a hair.

[III, 4247-4249]

Time is limited, and the abundant water is flowing away.
Drink, before you fall to pieces.
There is a famous conduit, full of the Water of Life:
draw the Water, so that you may become fruitful.
We are drinking the water of Khidr[19]
from the river of the speech of the saints:
Come, thirsty one!
Even if you don't see the water, as skillfully as a blind person,
bring the jug to the river and dip it in.

[III, 4300-4304]

One's inmost consciousness is like the root of a tree;
and just as the hard wood sprouts leaves
on the tree, in souls and minds
the leaves grow according to the root.
From the trees of faithfulness wings soar to heaven:
its root is fast in the earth and its branch is in the sky.[20]

[III, 4386-4388]

---

[19] Khidr is the immortal "Green Man" who appears as a guide to those who are worthy.
[20] Qur'an: Surah Ibrahim (Abraham), 14:24.

Surely there is a window from heart to heart:
they are not separate and far from each other.
Though two earthenware lamps are not joined,
their light mingles.
No lover seeks union without the beloved seeking;
but the love of lovers makes the body thin as a bowstring,
while the love of loved ones makes them shapely and pleasing.
When the lightning of love for the beloved
has shot into this heart, know that there is love in that heart.
When love for God has been doubled in your heart,
there is no doubt that God has love for you.

[III, 4391-4396]

No sound of clapping comes forth from only one hand.
The thirsty man is moaning, "O delicious water!"
The water is calling, "Where is the one who will drink me?"
This thirst in our souls is the magnetism of the Water:
We are Its, and It is ours.

[III, 4397-4399]

The desire in the female for the male
is so that they may perfect each other's work.
God put desire in man and woman
in order that the world should be preserved by this union.

[III, 4414-4416]

God instills the desire of every part for the other:
from their union, generation results.
And so night and day are in mutual embrace:
they appear to be opposites, even enemies,
but the truth they attend is one,
each desiring the other like kin,
for the perfection of their work.
Both serve one purpose, for without night,
human nature would receive no income:
what then could day expend?

[III, 4417-4420]

You make a hundred resolutions to journey somewhere:
He draws you somewhere else.
He turns the horse's bridle in every direction
that the untrained horse may gain knowledge of the rider.
The clever horse is well-paced
because it knows a rider is mounted upon it.
He fixed your heart on a hundred passionate desires,
disappointed you, and then broke your heart.
Since He broke the wings of your first intention,
how do you doubt the existence of the Wing-breaker?
Since His ordainment snapped the cord of contrivance,
how can you remain blind to His Command?

[III, 4456-4461]

Your resolutions and purposes now and then are fulfilled
so that through hope your heart might form another intention which He might once again destroy.
For if He were to keep you completely from success,
you would despair: how would the seed of expectation be sown?
If your heart did not sow that seed,
and then encounter barrenness,
how would it recognize its submission to Divine will?
By their failures lovers are made aware of their Lord.
Lack of success is the guide to Paradise:
Pay attention to the tradition,
"Paradise is encompassed with pain."[21]

[III, 4462-4467]

Come *against your will* is the toggle of the intelligent;
come willingly[22] is the spring-time
of those who have lost their hearts.

[III, 4472]

---

[21] *Hadith* of the Prophet Muhammad.

[22] Qur'an: Surah Fussilat (Clearly Spelled Out) 41:11.

The Prophet said, "Don't think of my ascension
as superior to that of Jonah:
mine was up to heaven; his was below into the belly of the fish,
but nearness to God is beyond calculation."
Nearness to God is neither up nor down:
to be near God is to escape the prison of existence.
What room has non-existence for "up" or "down"?
Non-existence has no "soon" or "far" or "late."
The laboratory and treasure house of God is in non-existence.
Since existence deludes you,
how will you know what non-existence is?

[III, 4512-4516]

The lover hotly pursues the beloved:
when the beloved comes, the lover is gone.
You are a lover of God, and God is such
that when He comes not a single hair of yours remains.
At that look of His a hundred like you vanish away.
I think you are in love with nothingness.
You are a shadow and in love with the sun.
When the sun comes, the shadow quickly disappears.

[III, 4620-463]

Such is the seeker of the court of God:
when God comes, the seeker is no more.
Although union with God is immortality upon immortality,
yet at first that immortality consists in dying to self.
The reflections that are seeking the Light
disappear when His Light appears.
How should reason remain when He bids it go?
Everything is perishing except His Face.[23]
Before His Face the existent and the non-existent perish:
existence in non-existence is truly a marvelous thing!
In this place of presence all minds are lost beyond control;
when the pen reaches this point, it breaks.

[III, 4658-63]

Love is a stranger to the two worlds:
in it are seventy-two madnesses.
It is hidden; only its bewilderment is manifest:
the soul of the spiritual sultan longs for it.
Love's religion is other than the seventy-two sects:
beside it the throne of kings is just a bandage.
In the moments of sema[24] Love's bard strikes up the melody:
"Servitude is bondage and power is a headache."
Then what is Love? The Sea of Not-Being:
there the foot of the intellect is shattered and can no longer swim.
Servitude and sovereignty are known:
the way of the lover is hidden by these two veils.

[III, 4719-4724]

---

[23] Qur'an: Surah Al-Qasas (The Story), 28:88.
[24] The occasion of listening to spiritual music.

Beware! Don't say, "Mind you, so and so sowed seed,
and then the locusts devoured it;
why should I bother sowing with such a risk?
Why should I let go of this corn-seed in my hand?"
Meanwhile, to your bewilderment,
one who did sow and labor
fills his barn with grain.
Since the lover patiently continued knocking at the door,
at last one day he gained an intimate meeting.

[III, 4800-4803]

In consequence of a fractured leg, God bestows a wing;
likewise from the depths of the pit, He opens a door of escape.
God said, "Don't consider whether you're up a tree or in a hole:
consider Me, for I am the Key of the Way."[25]

[III, 4808-4809]

[25] Hadith Qudsi, an extra-Qur'anic revelation.

Since you wish it so, God wishes it so;
God grants the desires of the devoted.
In the past it was as if he belonged to God,
but now "God belongs to him" has come in recompense.

[IV, 6-7]

The servant complains to God of pain:
in a hundred ways he moans.
God says, "But after all, grief and pain
have caused you to act rightly and call humbly upon Me;
complain instead of the bounty that befalls you
and takes you far from My door."
In reality every enemy of yours is your remedy:
he is an elixir, a gift, and one that seeks to win your heart;
for you flee from him into solitude
imploring God's help.

[IV, 91-95]

Your friends are really your enemies
as much as they keep you occupied with them
and take you away from the Presence.
There is an animal called a porcupine
which is made strong and big by the blows of the stick.
The more you beat it, the more it thrives.
Surely the true believer's soul is a porcupine,
for the blows of tribulation strengthen it.
For this reason, the trials and humiliation
laid upon the prophets is greater
than that laid upon all other creatures,
so that their souls become steadier than other souls;
for no other people have suffered such affliction.
The hide is burned by the treatment,
but it becomes supple like the leather of Ta'if;
and if the tanner didn't rub the acid solution into it,
it would only become fetid and repulsive.

[IV, 96-103]

A sober-minded man said to Jesus,
"What in this existence is the hardest to bear?"
"O dear soul," he replied, "the hardest is God's anger,
from which Hell is trembling as we are."
"And what is the protection against God's anger?"
Said Jesus, "To abandon your own anger at once."

[IV, 113-115]

When you have done wrong, be wary, don't be complacent,
for that evil is a seed God may cause to grow.
He covers it up for a while
and offers you a chance to feel sorrow and shame.
In the time of 'Umar, that Prince of the Faithful
turned a thief over for punishment.
The thief cried out, "O Prince of the land,
this is my first offence, have mercy!"
"God forbid," said 'Umar, "that the Merciful
should inflict punishment the first time.
His Mercy veils the sinner many times;
until His Justice can no longer be withheld.
At last both these attributes are displayed:
the former to bring hope and the latter to deter."

[IV, 165-171]

In marriage both partners must be equal,
otherwise it will pinch, and their happiness will not endure.

[IV, 197]

The one who is overwhelmed in Our grace is not compelled;
no, he is one who freely chooses devotion to Us.
In truth the aim of free will
is that free will should be lost.

[IV, 401-402]

Know that between the Faithful is an ancient union.
The Faithful are numerous, but the Faith is one:
their bodies are numerous, but their soul is one.
Besides the understanding which is in the ox and the ass,
the human being has another intelligence and soul.
Again, in the saint, the owner of Divine breath,
there is a soul and intelligence other than human.
The souls of wolves and dogs are separate, every one,
but the souls of the Lions of God are in union.

[IV, 407-410; 414]

The light of the senses and spirit of our ancestors
doesn't perish like the grass,
but, like the stars and moonbeams,
they vanish in the radiance of the Sun.
It's like the naked man who jumped into the water,
so that he might escape from the hornets' stings:
the hornets circled above him, and whenever he put out his head
they would not spare him.
The water is recollection of God,
and the hornet is the thought, during this time,
of such-and-such a woman or man.
Hold your breath in the water of remembrance,
so you may be freed from old thoughts and temptations.
After that, you will assume the nature of that pure water,
entirely from head to foot.
As the noxious hornet flees from the water,
so will it be afraid of approaching you.
After that be far from the water, if you wish;
for in your inmost soul you are of the same nature as the water.
Those persons then who have passed from the world
are not non-existent but are absorbed in the attributes of God,
even as the star disappears in the presence of the sun.

[IV, 432-433; 435-443]

When Solomon went into the temple every morning
to guide the servants of God,
he would exhort them sometimes by speech and melody,
sometimes by action—I mean, a bowing or a prayer.
The exhortation of act draws people more powerfully,
for it reaches the soul of those who hear,
as well as those who are deaf.
In action the conceit of authority is less than in words,
and action makes a stronger impression on those who follow.

[IV, 483-485]

In form you are the microcosm;
in reality you are the macrocosm.

[IV, 521]

The Prophet said, "I am like an Ark in the Flood of Time.
I and my companions are like the Ship of Noah:
whoever clings to us will gain spiritual graces."
When you are with the Shaikh you are far removed from evil:
day and night you are a traveler in a ship.
You are under the protection of a life-giving spirit:
you are asleep in the ship and proceeding on the way.
Don't break with the prophet of your day;
don't rely on your own skill and footsteps.
Lion though you are, to go on the way without a guide
is arrogant, foolish, and contemptible.
Step aboard the ship and set sail,
like the soul going towards the soul's Beloved.
Without hands or feet, travel toward Timelessness
just as spirits flee from non-existence.

[IV, 538-543; 557-558]

The bird tempted by the bait may still be on the roof,
but with wings outspread, it is already imprisoned in the trap.
If with all its soul it has given its heart to the bait,
consider it caught, even though it may still appear to be free.
Consider the looks it gives to the bait to be
the knots it is tying on its own legs.
The bait says, "You may be stealing looks away from me,
but know that I am stealing patience and constancy away from you."

[IV, 620-623]

If you don't have sovereignty over your own beard,
how will you exercise sovereignty over good and evil?
Without your wish, your beard grows white:
be ashamed of your beard, you with your self-serving dreams.
God is the Owner of the Kingdom:
whoever lays his head before Him,
will receive a hundred kingdoms without the terrestrial world;
but the inward savour of a single prostration before God
will be sweeter to you than a hundred empires:
then you will cry humbly, "I want no kingdoms
except the kingdom of that prostration."

[IV, 662-666]

In the well of this world there are optical illusions,
the least of which is that stones appear to be gold.
To the fantasy of children playing
the debris with which they play appears as gold and riches.
Yet through the alchemy God's gnostics practice,
to their eyes, mines of gold become worthless.

[IV, 675-677]

Sema[26] is the food of the lovers of God,
for within it is the taste of tranquility of mind.
From the hearing of certain sounds,
visions gain strength
until they become actual forms within the imagination.
The fire of love is intensified by melodies.

[IV, 742-744]

If you are born of Adam, sit like him
and behold all his progeny within yourself.
What is in the jar that is not also in the river?
What is in the house that is not also in the city?
This world is a jar, and the heart-spirit is like the river;
this world is the chamber, and the spirit is the wondrous city.

[IV, 809-811]

---

[26] Sema is an occasion for whirling and listening to spiritual music.

Our body is our veil in the world:
we are like a sea hidden beneath a straw.

[IV, 823]

Although this reed pen is in fact insensible,
of a different substance than the writer,
yet it is an intimate friend.
Likewise, every tool of a craftsman, though lifeless,
is the familiar friend of the Human spirit.

[IV, 875-876]

Even when luck is with you and you're powerful,
still, Prosperity is other than you are:
one day it departs and leaves you poor.
O you who've been chosen, be your own good fortune!
When you have become your own wealth, O man of Reality,
then how will you, who are Prosperity, lose yourself?
How will you lose yourself, O man of good qualities,
when your Essence is your wealth and your kingdom?

[IV, 1109-1112]

God, You who know all that is hidden,
You who speak with compassion,
don't hide from us the errors of our wrong pursuits—
nor reveal to us the lack within the good we try to do,
lest we become disgusted and lose the heart
to journey on this Path.

[IV, 1353-1354]

When you say, "I'm ignorant: teach me,"
such honesty is better than a false reputation.
Learn from your father Adam, O clear-browed man:
he said, "*O our Lord*" and "*We have done wrong.*"[27]
He made no excuses, nor did he invent lies,
nor did he lift up the banner of evasion.

[IV,1388-1390]

Love is a ship for the elect:
it is deliverance from disaster.
Sell intelligence and buy bewilderment:
your intelligence may be opinion,
while bewilderment may be naked vision.
Sacrifice your understanding in the presence of Muhammad:
say, *God suffices me.*[28]

[IV, 1406-1408]

---

[27] Qur'an: Surah Al-Anbiya (The Prophets), 21:97.

[28] *Hadith* of Muhammad: God is sufficient for me (*hasbiya 'llah*).

Sacrifice your intellect in love for the Friend:
for anyway, intellects come from where He is.
The spiritually intelligent have sent their intellects back to Him:
only the fool remains where the Beloved is not.
If from bewilderment, this intellect of yours flies out of your head,
every tip of your hair will become a new knowing.
In the presence of the Beloved, the brain needn't labor;
for there the brain and intellect spontaneously produce
fields and orchards of spiritual knowledge.
If you turn towards that field, you will hear a subtle discourse;
in that oasis your palm tree will freshen and flourish.

[IV, 1424-1428]

Listen, *stand up in prayer during the night,*[29]
for you are a candle,
and at night a candle stands and burns.

[IV, 1456]

---

[29] Qur'an: Surah Al-Muzzamil (The Enwrapped One), 73:20.

The body is like a letter:
look into it and see whether it's worthy to be read by the King.
Go into a corner, open the letter, and read what is in it,
see whether its words are suitable for royalty.
If it isn't suitable, tear it to pieces,
write another letter, and remedy the fault.
But don't think it's easy to open the letter of the body;
otherwise everyone would readily discover the secret of the heart.
How difficult it is to open that letter!
It's only for the strong, not for those playing games.

[IV, 1564-1568]

If you're lugging a heavy bag,
don't fail to look inside it
to see whether what is inside is bitter or sweet.
If it's really worth bringing along, bring it;
otherwise, empty your sack
and redeem yourself from fruitless effort and disgrace.
Only put into your sack
that which is worth bringing to a righteous sovereign.

[IV, 1574-1577]

Everything in the world draws something to itself:
infidelity draws the faithless,
and goodness, the one who is rightly guided.
Both magnet and amber attract:
whether you are iron or straw, you will be drawn.
If you are straw, you will be drawn to the amber;
and if you are iron, you will be pulled to the magnet.
When anyone is not associated with the good,
he inevitably becomes a neighbor to the corrupt.

[IV, 1633-1636]

If in the darkness of ignorance,
you don't recognize a person's true nature,
look to see whom he has chosen for his leader.

[IV, 1640]

Charity for God's sake has a hundred signs within the heart—
the good deed, a hundred tokens.
Though in charity riches are consumed,
a hundred lives come to the heart in return.
A sowing of pure seeds in God's earth, and then no income! Impossible.

[IV, 1757-1759]

The days of the body are increased by the spirit:
look what becomes of the body when the spirit departs.
The range of the body is an arm's length or two,
yet your spirit soars in the infinite.
Within the spirit's imagining,
it's only half a step to Baghdad or Samarkand.
The white of your eye is a coin's weight,
but the light of its spirit reaches the heights of the sky.
In a dream, without this eye, the light sees:
without this light what would the eye be but ruined?

[IV, 1881-1885]

There are two kinds of intelligence.
One is like that acquired by a child at school
from books and teachers, new ideas and memorization.
Your intelligence may become superior to others,
but retaining all that knowledge is a burden.
You who are so busy searching for knowledge
must be a preserving tablet, but the preserved tablet
is the one who has gone beyond all this.
For the other kind of intelligence is the gift of God:
its fountain is deep within the soul.
When the water of God-given knowledge surges from the breast,
it never stagnates or becomes impure.
And if its way to the outside is blocked, what harm is there?
For it flows continually from the house of the heart.
The acquired intelligence is like the conduits
which run into the house from the streets:
if those pipes become blocked, the house is bereft of water.
Seek the fountain within yourself.

[IV, 1960-1968]

Whoever is sitting with friends
is in the midst of a flower garden,
though he may be in the fire.
Whoever sits with an enemy is in the fire,
even though he is in the midst of a garden.

[IV, 1976-1978]

Whoever is fond of training,
will not escape the kicks.

[IV, 2008]

Silence is the sea, and speech is like the river.
The sea is seeking you: don't seek the river.
Don't turn your head away from the signs offered by the sea.

[IV, 2062-2063]

When you are seated beside your beloved,
send away the go-between.
For the one who is no longer a child,
the letter and the go-between are a nuisance.
The mature one reads letters,
but only for the purpose of teaching others;
he utters words, but only for the purpose of making others understand.
To repeat hearsay in the presence of those who have vision,
only proves your lack of awareness.
In the presence of one who sees, silence is to your advantage:
for this reason God proclaimed, *Be silent.*

[IV, 2068-2072]

Every moment in which you enjoy union with the Beloved,
is like being at the edge of the roof.
You may tremble for fear of losing that delight:
conceal that moment like a treasure, don't display it.
Don't let calamity suddenly befall your love; pay attention,
go vigilantly into that place of ambush.
The spirit's fear of loss at that moment of enjoyment
is a sign that the descent has begun.
Even if you don't see that mysterious roof edge,
the spirit sees it and shudders.
Every sudden chastisement that has come to pass
has taken place on the edge of the turret of enjoyment.
Indeed there is no fall except from the edge of the roof.

[IV, 2147-2153]

If you can't bear the bite of a flea,
how will you endure the bite of a snake?
In appearance I am ruining your work,
but in reality I am making a thorn into a rose garden.

[IV, 2339-2340]

Seeing a man who was tilling the earth,
a fool, unable to control himself, cried out,
"Why are you ruining this soil?"
"Fool," said the man, "leave me alone:
try to recognize the difference
between tending the soil and wasting it.
How will this soil become a rose garden
until it is disturbed and overturned?"

[IV, 2341-2345]

When a tailor cuts the cloth for a garment piece by piece,
does anyone strike him,
saying, "Why have you torn this choice satin?"
Whenever the builders repair an old building,
don't they first ruin the old one?
Likewise the carpenter, the blacksmith, and the butcher—
with them too there is destruction before restoration.
The pounding of the myrobalan
becomes the means of restoring the body to health.
Unless you crush the wheat in the mill,
how will there be bread on your table?

[IV, 2348-2353]

When you whirl, your eye sees the room whirling, too.
If you sail in a ship over the sea,
it seems the seashore is running past.
If your heart is oppressed with struggle,
the whole atmosphere of the world feels tight;
but if you are happy as your friends would wish,
this world seems to be a garden of roses.

[IV, 2369-2372]

How many have gone as far as Syria and Iraq
and have seen nothing but unbelief and hypocrisy;
and how many have gone as far as India and Herat
and seen nothing but selling and buying;
and how many have gone as far as Turkestan and China
and seen nothing but deceit and trickery!
If the traveler has no object of perception except external sensations,
let him seek through all the world, he will see nothing of spirit.
If a cow suddenly came into Baghdad
and passed from this side of the city to the other,
of all its pleasures and joys and delights,
it will see nothing but the rind of a watermelon.

[IV, 2373-2378]

God gave relationship to the unrelated.

[IV, 2408]

God has given you the polishing instrument, Reason,
so that by means of it the surface of the heart may be made resplendent.

[IV, 2475]

The human being is like the water of the river:
when it becomes turbid, you can't see to the bottom.
The bottom of the river is full of jewels and pearls:
pay attention, don't stir up the water,
for originally it's pure and free from pollution.
The human spirit resembles the atmosphere:
when air is mixed with dust, it veils the sky,
and prevents the eye from seeing the sun;
but when the dust is gone, the air once again becomes pure.
Despite your complete darkness, God may offer you visions,
that you might find the way of deliverance.

[IV, 2482-2486]

By the mercy of God Paradise has eight doors—
one of those is the door of repentance, child.
All the others are sometimes open, sometimes shut;
but the door of repentance is never closed.
Come seize the opportunity: the door is open;
carry your baggage there at once.

[IV, 2506-2508]

Demolish the house, for a hundred thousand houses
may be made from this carnelian.
The treasure lies beneath the house, and there is no other way:
don't be afraid of destroying the house and don't stand still,
for from one treasure in hand it is possible to build
a thousand houses without suffering toil and pain.
In the end this house will fall of itself into ruin,
and the treasure beneath it will certainly be uncovered;
But then the treasure won't be yours,
since your soul receives that divine gift as wages for destroying the house.
When it hasn't done the work, it earns no wages:
There is nothing for the Human being hereafter
but recompense for that which she has wrought here.[30]

[IV, 2540-2545]

[30] Qur'an: Surah Al-Imran (The House of Imran), 3:25.

Listen, O drop, give yourself up without regret,
and in exchange gain the Ocean.
Listen, O drop, bestow upon yourself this honor,
and in the arms of the Sea be secure.
Who indeed should be so fortunate?
An Ocean wooing a drop!
In God's name, in God's name, sell and buy at once!
Give a drop, and take this Sea full of pearls.

[IV, 2619-2622]

When Satan sees, to the left or right, anyone who is perfect,
he becomes ill with envy,
for every miserable wretch whose stack has been burnt
is unwilling that anyone else's candle should be lighted.
Pay attention, work on perfecting yourself,
so that the perfection of others may not grieve you.
Beg of God the removal of envy,
that God may deliver you from externals,
and bestow upon you an inward occupation,
which will absorb you
so that your attention is not drawn outward.

[IV, 2678-2682]

5/31

Listen my heart, don't be deceived by every intoxication:
Jesus is intoxicated with God, the ass is intoxicated with barley.

[IV, 2691]

6/1

The sword is for the one whose proud neck is held high;
no blow falls on the shadow thrown flat upon the ground.

[IV, 2759]

6/2

To exalt oneself is to claim partnership with God.
Unless you have died and become living through Him,
you are an enemy seeking to hold the power.
But when you have come to live through God,
that which you have become is in truth He:
it is no longer copartnership, but absolute Unity.

[IV, 2765-2767]

God spoke to Moses by inspiration of the heart,
saying, "O chosen one, I love you."
Moses said, "O Bountiful One,
tell me what disposition in me is the cause of that,
so that I might increase it."
God said, "You are like a child in the presence of its mother:
when she reprimands it, it still holds tightly to her.
It doesn't even know that there is anyone in the world except her:
it is afflicted with sorrow by her
but also intoxicated with joy by her.
If its mother gives it a slap,
still it comes to its mother and clings to her.
It doesn't seek help from anyone but her:
she is all its evil and its good.
Your heart, likewise, in good or evil straits
never turns away from Me.
In your sight all besides Me are as stones and lumps of earth,
whether they be young or old.
Just as *You do we worship* in yearning entreaty,
so in difficulty *we ask help of none but You.*[31]

[IV, 2921-2929]

---

[31] Qur'an: Surah al-Fatihah (The Opening) 1:5.

614 In battle the cowardly out of fear for their lives
have chosen the means of retreat,
while the courageous, also from fear for their lives,
have charged towards the ranks of the enemy.
Heroes are borne onward by their fear and pain;
from fear, too, the human being of weak spirit dies within.

[IV, 2917-2919]

615 Your true substance is concealed in falsehood,
like the taste of butter in buttermilk.
Your falsehood is this perishable body;
your truth is that exalted spirit.
For many years, this buttermilk of the body,
is visible and manifest, while the butter, which is the spirit,
is perishing and ignored within it—
until God sends a prophet, a chosen servant,
a shaker of the buttermilk in the churn,
who skillfully shakes it, so that you might know
your true self which was hidden.

[IV, 3030-3034]

Hand is above hand, child, in skill and in strength, 6/6
up to the Essence of God,
The ultimate end of all hands is the Hand of God:
the ultimate end of all torrents is undoubtedly the sea.
From it the clouds take their origin,
and in it, too, the torrent has an end.

[IV, 3162-3164]

Many set out from the very spot 6/7
where the object of their quest is to be found.
The far sight and boasting of the sleeper is of no use;
it is nothing but a fantasy—don't be caught by it.
You are sleepy, but at least sleep on the Way:
for God's sake, sleep on the Way of God,
that by chance a traveler on the Way may stumble upon you
and tear you from the fantasies of your slumber.
The sleeper dreams of the dire pangs of thirst,
while the water is *nearer to him than the neck vein.*[32]

[IV, 3234-3237; 3241]

---

[32] Qur'an: Surah Qaf, 50:16.

6/18

The whole world is the unfolding of Universal Reason
which is the father of whoever takes the Divine Word as a guide.
When anyone shows extreme ingratitude to Universal Reason,
the whole form of the universe appears to him to snarl.
Make peace with this father, stop rebelling,
that the water and clay of this world
might appear to you as a carpet of gold.
Then you will live in the Resurrection:
heaven and earth will be transfigured before you.
Since I am always at peace with the father,
this world looks to me like Paradise.
At every moment a new form appears and a new beauty,
so that from seeing new visions, boredom dies.
I see the world as full of bounty—
the waters constantly gushing from the springs.
The voice of their water comes to my ear,
and my inner consciousness is drunk with the sound.

[IV, 3259-3266]

Your intelligence is spread over a hundred "important" affairs,
over thousands of desires and concerns great and small.
You must unite the scattered parts by means of love,
so that you may become as sweet as Damascus and Samarkand.
When you have become united,
particle by particle, from out of perplexity,
then it is possible to stamp the King's seal upon you.

[IV, 3288-3290]

The flash of lightning is not to light the way,
but a command to the cloud to weep.
The lightning of the mind is for the sake of weeping,
so that what doesn't exist may weep, longing for true existence.
The child's mind tells it, "You must go to school";
but it cannot be the teacher.
The sick man's mind tells him to see a doctor,
but it cannot cure him.

[IV, 3320-3323]

God drove the devils from His place of watch;
He drove the particular intellect from its autonomy,
saying, "Don't domineer; you are not autonomous—
no, you are the pupil of the heart and created to learn from it.
Go to the heart, go, for you are a part of the heart:
pay attention, for you are a slave of that just King."
To be His slave is better than being a sovereign,
for only Satan says, "*I am better.*"[33]
See the distinction and prefer, O prisoner,
the servanthood of Adam to the pride of Iblis.[34]

[IV, 3339-3343]

Rub your eyes with the dust of every mature one:
that salve will both burn the eye and do it good.
The eye of the camel is luminous
because the camel eats thorns to increase the light of its eye.

[IV, 3375-3376]

[33] Qur'an: Surah al-A'Raf (The Faculty of Discernment) 7:12.
[34] The Devil.

The difference between truth and falsehood becomes visible
the moment the collyrium of grace clears the eye;
otherwise, dung and musk seem the same
to one whose nose is clogged.
To cure boredom he picks up something to read,
neglecting the Word of the Almighty,
that by means of some entertaining article
he may quell the painful fire and anxiety.
Either pure water or urine would work to put out the fire.
But if you really come to know this pure water,
the Word of God which is of the spirit,
all distress will vanish from your soul,
and your heart will find its way to the rose garden,
for everyone who catches a scent of the mystery of revelation
discovers a spiritual orchard with a running brook.

[IV, 3464-3472]

God said, "I am All-Sufficing: I will give you all good,
with no intervening cause, without any mediator.
I am All-sufficing: I will give you fullness without bread;
without spring I will give you narcissi and wild-roses.
I will instruct you without books or teachers.
I am All-Sufficing: I will heal you without medicine,
I will make the grave and the pit open into a spacious playing field."

[IV, 3516-3520]

To the Prophet, this world is plunged in glorification of God,
while to us it is heedless.
To his eye this world is filled with abundant love;
to the eyes of others it is inert and lifeless.
To his eye, valley and hill are in fluid motion:
he hears subtle discourses from sod and bricks.
To the vulgar, this whole world is a dead thing in chains:
I have never seen a veil of blindness more amazing than this.

[IV, 3532-3535]

No wonder the soul doesn't remember its ancient home,
its original dwelling and place of birth,
since the sleep of this world covers it as clouds hide the stars.
It has walked through so many cities,
and the dust hasn't yet been wiped from its perception.
It hasn't yet worked to purify its heart and behold the past,
that its heart might peek from the aperture of mystery
and see its beginning with open eyes.

[IV, 3632-3636]

Just as the human being does not recall its earlier forms of intelligence,
this present intelligence also must be left behind and forgotten
in order to escape this self-serving greed
and witness a hundred thousand new forms of intelligence.
Though one falls asleep and becomes oblivious of the past,
how can they leave him in that state of self-forgetfulness?
From that sleep they will bring him back again to wakefulness,
to mock at his present state, saying,
"What was that sorrow I was suffering in my sleep?
How did I forget the states of truth, of real experience?"

And so with this world, which is the sleeper's dream:
the sleeper imagines it is enduring,
until suddenly the dawn of Death arises,
and she is delivered from the obscurity of distorted opinion.
She will laugh at those sorrows of hers
when she sees her permanent abode and resting place.
Everything good or evil that you see in your sleep
will be manifest, one by one, on the Day of Reckoning.
That which you did during your sleep in this present world
will become manifest to you at the time of wakening.
Take care not to imagine that the hurtful acts made during this sleep
will find no interpretation there.

[IV, 3648-3652; 3654-3659]

In real existence there is only unity.

[IV, 3829]

The religious law is like a candle showing the way.
Unless you gain possession of the candle,
there is no wayfaring;
and when you have come on to the way,
your wayfaring is the Path;
and when you have reached the journey's end,
that is the Truth. So it has been said,
"If realities were manifest, religious laws would not exist."

[Prologue]

Till the cloud weeps, how should the garden smile?
The weeping of the cloud and the burning of the sun
are the pillars of this world: twist these two strands together.
Since the searing heat of the sun and the moisture of the clouds
keep the world fresh and sweet,
keep the sun of your intelligence burning bright
and your eye glistening with tears.

[V, 134; 138-139; 141-142]

It is said, *Lend unto God,*[35]
so give a loan of the leafage of this body,
that a garden may grow in your heart.
Give a loan, diminish the body's food,
so you may see what the eye has never seen.
When the body becomes empty,
God fills it with musk and luminous pearls.

[V, 146-148]

The water says to those who are dirty, "Listen, come here,
for my nature has partaken of the nature of God.
I can accept all your foulness
and render even a demon as pure as an angel.
When I become filthy, I return to the Source of the source of purity.
There I pull the filthy shirt off my head,
and He bestows upon me a clean one once again.
Such is His work, and my work is the same:
the Sustainer of all created beings[36] beautifies the world."

[V, 204-208]

---

[35] Qur'an: Surah Al-Hadid (Iron), 57:11.
[36] Qur'an: Surah An-Nas (Mankind), 114:1.

Though Light is the food of the spirit and spiritual vision,
the body also partakes of it.
If your belly is greedy, turn away from the world;
the only way is to change what you eat.
You whose heart is sick, turn to the remedy:
the entire diet is a change of attitude.
You who are kept in pawn to food,
you can be free if you suffer yourself to be weaned.
Truly in hunger there is abundant nourishment:
search after it diligently and cherish the hope of finding it.
Feed on the Light, be like the eye,
be in harmony with the angels, O best of humankind.
Like the Angel, make glorification of God your sustenance.

[V, 288; 293-298]

Love is whispering into my ear,
"To be a prey is better than to be a hunter.
Make yourself My fool:
renounce the high estate of the sun and become a speck!
Come dwell at My door and be homeless:
don't pretend to be a candle, be a moth,
so you may taste the savor of Life
and contemplate the sovereignty hidden in servitude."

[V, 411-414]

If you are wise like the Friend of God,
the fire is water to you, especially this fire of Love,
which is the soul of all waters . . . and you are a moth.
But the ignorant moth behaves differently than we do:
it sees the light and ends up in the fire.
The heart of the mystic sees fire and goes into the Light.
A fire has been made to look like water,
while within the apparent fire is a real fountain.

[V, 438; 442–443; 445]

The generous Prophet said it so well:
"A grain of intelligence is better for you
than fasting and the performance of ritual prayer,"
because intelligence is the substance, the others are contingent:
these two are made obligatory for those who possess the complement,
in order that the mirror might shine brightly.
Purity comes to the heart from piety.
But if the mirror is fundamentally flawed,
it takes the polisher a long time to restore it to purity.
While in the case of the fine mirror,
which is like good soil for planting,
a little polishing is all that's needed.

[V, 454–458]

Never, O wolf, play at being a fox,
performing service in order to gain power;
rush into the fire like a moth:
don't hoard service, play for love!

[V, 472-473]

After you've become nothing, you needn't fear the anvil:
take lessons every morning from absolute nothingness.

[V, 532]

Suppose you know the definitions of all substances
and their derivatives,
what good is this to you?
Know the true definition of yourself.
That is indispensable.
Then, when you know your own definition, flee from it,
that you may attain to the One who cannot be defined,
O sifter of the dust.

[V, 564-565]

God has said, "*Spend*"[37]; so earn something,
since there can be no expenditure without income.
Although He used the word, *Spend* absolutely,
read it, "Earn, then spend."

[V, 579-580]

Love is the flame which, when it blazes,
consumes everything other than the Beloved.
The lover wields the sword of *Nothingness*[38]
in order to dispatch all but God:
consider what remains after *Nothing*.
There remains *but God*: all the rest is gone.
Praise to you, O mighty Love, destroyer of all other "gods."

[V, 588-590]

---

37 Qur'an: Surah Al-Hadid (Iron), 57:7.

38 The *"la"* of "La illaha il Allah." (There are *no* gods but God.) Qur'an 3:62.

The wise Prophet has said that no one who dies
and dismounts from the steed of the body
feels grief on account of departure and death,
but only for missed opportunities and having failed in good works.
Truly everyone who dies wishes
that their arrival at their destination might have come sooner:
the wicked, in order that their wickedness might have been less;
and the devoted,
in order that they might have reached home more quickly.

[V, 604-607]

When through spiritual poverty someone is graced with nonexistence,
like Muhammad, he loses his shadow.
Fana[39] graced the Prophet who said, "Poverty is my pride."[40]
He became shadowless like the flame of a candle.
When the candle has become entirely flame from head to foot,
a shadow has no way to approach it.
The waxen candle fled from itself and its shadow into radiance
for the sake of the One by whom it was made.
God said, "I molded you for the sake of *fana*."
It replied, "And so I took refuge in *fana*."

[V, 672-676]

---

[39] Disappearance of the individual self in the being of God.
[40] *Hadith*, a saying of the Prophet Muhammad.

On Resurrection Day, the sun and moon are released from service:
and the eye beholds the Source of their radiance,
then it discerns the permanent possession from the loan,
and this passing caravan from the abiding home.
If for a while a wet nurse is needed,
Mother, quickly return us to your breast.
I don't want a nurse; my Mother is more fair.
I am like Moses whose nurse and Mother were the very same.

[V, 698; 701]

The mystery of "Poverty is my pride"[41] is sublime:
it cautions you to take refuge from the covetous
with the One who is Self-Sufficient.
Treasures are buried in ruined, forgotten places,
hidden from the greed of those who dwell in affluence.
If you can't tear out your own beautiful feathers,
go, adopt a life of solitude;
don't let yourself be dissipated by others.
For you are both the morsel of food and the eater of that morsel:
you are the consumer and the consumed. Understand this, dear one!

[V, 715-718]

[41] *Hadith*, a saying of the Prophet Muhammad.

Every fantasy devours another fantasy:
one thought feeds on another.
You can't be delivered from fantasy
or fall asleep to escape from it altogether.
Your thoughts are like hornets, and your sleep is like the water
in which you are plunged: when you awake, the hornets return,
and many hornet-like fantasies fly in
and draw you now this way and then that way.
This mental fantasy is the least of the devourers:
the Almighty knows how great the others are.
Listen, flee from the hordes of devourers
towards the One who has said, "*We are your Protector*"[42];
or if you can't hasten towards the Protector Himself,
towards the one who has gained that power of protection.

[V, 729-735]

A human being is united
with the one whom that being has made a friend.
That friend is with you in this world and in the other world;
this is the meaning of the *hadith*[43] of sweet-natured Muhammad,
who said, "In Paradise we will be with those whom we love."
The heart is not severed from its focus of desire.

[V, 745-747]

---

[42] Qur'an: Surah Al-Imran (The House of Imran), 3:150.
[43] A saying of the Prophet.

The greed of hunting makes one oblivious to being a prey:
the hunter tries to win hearts, though he has lost his own.
Don't be inferior to a bird in your seeking:
for even a sparrow sees what is *before and behind.*[44]
When the bird approaches the bait,
at that moment it turns its head several times to the rear and the front,
as if to say, "Is there a hunter somewhere near,
Should I be careful? Should I touch this food?"

[V, 752-755]

Life without repentance is spiritual agony;
to be absent from God is immediate death.
Life and deathboth are sweet with God's presence:
without God even the Water of Life is fire.

[V, 770-771]

[44] Qur'an: Surah Al-Baqarah (The Cow), 2:255.

O You who have transmuted one clod of earth into gold,
and another into the Father of mankind,
Your generous work is the transmutation of essences;
my work is mostly forgetfulness and mistakes.
Transmute my mistakes and forgetfulness into knowledge:
With my imperfect nature, turn me into patience and forbearance.

[V, 780-782]

The Prophet said, "God doesn't pay attention to your outer form:
so in your improvising, seek the owner of the Heart."
God says, "I regard you through the owner of the Heart,
not because of prostrations in prayer or the giving of wealth in charity."[45]
The owner of the Heart becomes a six-faced mirror:
through him God looks out upon all the six directions.

[V, 869-870; 874]

---

[45] *Hadith Qudsi*, an extra-Qur'anic revelation.

If a wealthy person brings a hundred sacks of gold,
God will only say,
"Bring the Heart, you who are bent double.
If the Heart is pleased with you, I am pleased;
and if the Heart is opposed to you, I am opposed.
I don't pay attention to "you;" I look to the heart:
bring it, poor soul, as a gift to My door!
It's relation to you is also mine:
Paradise is at the feet of mothers."[46]
The heart is the mother and father and origin of all creatures:
the one who knows the heart from the skin is blessed.
You will say, "Look, I have brought a heart to You":
God will respond, "Qutu is full of these hearts.
Bring the heart that is the axis of the world
and the soul of the soul of the soul of Adam."
The Ruler of all hearts is waiting
for a heart filled with light and goodness.

[V, 881-888]

[46] *Hadith*, a saying of the Prophet Muhammad.

Over the years that soft moon-like face
becomes like the back of a Libyan lizard,
and that head crowned with fair hair grows ugly and bald.
Truly these are signs of pain and decay, each a messenger of death.
But if your physician is the Light of God,
no loss or crushing blow is suffered from fever or old age.
The one without Light is an orchard without fruit,
which the autumn will bring to ruin.

[V, 968-969; 973-974; 977]

Moment by moment you await understanding and spiritual perception,
peace and good to arrive from non-existence.
Non-existence, then, is God's factory
from which He continually produces goods.
He has caused what is non-existent to appear magnificently existent,
while the truly existent He has caused to appear as non-existent.
He has hidden the Sea, yet made the foam visible;
He has concealed the Wind, but displayed the dust.
The dust whirls in the air higher than a minaret:
does it rise by itself? You see the dust borne high,
but the Wind you don't see, although you can surmise it.
You see the white-capped waves tumbling in every direction,
but without the Sea the foam has no way to move.
You see the foam by sense perception and the Sea by induction:
just as speech is manifest and thought is hidden.

[V, 1022; 1024-1031]

The servant for whom the world lovingly wept
the world now rejects: what did he do wrong?
His crime was that he put on borrowed clothes
and pretended he owned them.
We take them back, in order that he may know for sure
that the stock is Ours and the well-dressed are only borrowers;
that he may know that those robes were a loan,
a ray from the Sun of Being.
All that beauty, power, virtue, and excellence
have arrived here from the Sun of Excellence.
They, the light of that Sun, turn back again,
like the stars, from these bodily walls.
When the Sunbeam has returned home,
every wall is left darkened and black.
That which amazed you in the faces of the fair
is the Light of the Sun reflected in the three-colored glass.
The glasses of diverse hue cause the Light to appear colored to us.
When the many-colored glasses are no more,
then the colorless Light amazes you.
Make it your habit to behold the Light without the glass,
so that when the glass is shattered you may not be left blind.

[V, 981-991]

This world is a sorcerer,
and we are the merchants who buy
yards of measured moonbeams.
When it takes the money of our life,
our purse is emptied, and we are left without linen.
You must recite, *Say, I take refuge,*
crying "O You who are One, come,
save me from *those who cast knotted spells.*[47]
But invoke Him with the tongue of deeds as well,
for the tongue of words is weak.

[V, 1039-1042; 1044]

In this world you have three companions:
one is faithful, the others are treacherous.
The latter are friends and possessions;
the faithful one is excellence in deeds.
Your wealth won't come with you out of your palace;
your friend will come, but only as far as the grave.
When the day of doom comes to meet you,
your friend will say, "I've come this far, but no farther.
I will stand a while at your grave."
Your deeds alone are faithful: make them your refuge,
for they alone will accompany you into the depths of the tomb.

[V, 1045-1050]

[47] Qur'an: Surah Al-Falaq (The Rising Dawn), 113:1,4.

Strip the raiment of pride from your body:
in learning, put on the garment of humility.
Soul receives from soul the knowledge of humility,
not from books or speech.
Though mysteries of spiritual poverty are within the seeker's heart,
she doesn't yet possess knowledge of those mysteries.
Let her wait until her heart expands and fills with Light:
God said, "*Did We not expand your breast. . .?*[48]
For We have put illumination there,
We have put the expansion into your heart."
When you are a source of milk, why are you milking another?
An endless fountain of milk is within you:
why are you seeking milk with a pail?
You are a lake with a channel to the Sea:
be ashamed to seek water from a pool;
For *did We not expand. . .?* Again, don't you possess the expansion?
Why are you going about like a beggar?
Contemplate the expansion of the heart within you,
that you may not be reproached with, *Do you not see?*[49]

[V, 1061; 1064-1072]

[48] Qur'an: Surah Ash-Sharh (The Opening of the Heart), 94:1.
[49] Qur'an: Surah Adh-Dhariyat (The Dust-Scattering Winds) 51:21.

There's a basket full of loaves on your head,
yet you're begging for crusts of bread from door to door.
Pay attention to your own head, abandon giddyness.
Why are you knocking at every other door?
Go, knock at the door of your own heart.

[V, 1073-1074]

What is justice? Giving water to trees.
What is injustice? To give water to thorns.
Justice consists in bestowing bounty in its proper place,
not on every root that will absorb water.

[V, 1089-1090]

Are you fleeing from Love because of a single humiliation?
What do you know of Love except the name?
Love has a hundred forms of pride and disdain,
and is gained by a hundred means of persuasion.
Since Love is loyal, it purchases one who is loyal:
it has no interest in a disloyal companion.
The human being resembles a tree; its root is a covenant with God:
that root must be cherished with all one's might.
A weak covenant is a rotten root, without grace or fruit.
Though the boughs and leaves of the date palm are green,
greenness brings no benefit if the root is corrupt.
If a branch is without green leaves, yet has a good root,
a hundred leaves will put forth their hands in the end.

[V, 1163-1169]

Abandon the dry prayer of words,
for the tree presupposes the scattering of seeds.
Yet even if you have no seed, due to your prayer,
God will bestow upon you a palm tree
saying, "How well did he labor!"
Like Mary—she had heart-felt pain, but no seed:
an artful One made that withered palm-tree green for her sake.
Because that noble Lady was loyal to God,
God fulfilled a hundred desires without desire on her part.

[V, 1188-1191]

The precedence of Mercy over Wrath exists as a fact, youthful one:
Mercy has eternally been predominant in the nature of God.
And those chosen as servants by necessity possess this disposition:
their water-skins are filled from the water of the Stream.
The Messenger of God and the mystic Guide
have said that people follow the ways of their leaders.

[V, 1591-1593]

God's cruelty is better than a hundred kindnesses of ours:
to withhold the soul from God only increases the agony.
God's worst cruelty is better than the generosity of both worlds:
how extraordinary is *the Sustainer of created beings,*[50]
and how beautiful the help given!
In such cruelty there are secret kindnesses:
to surrender the soul for the sake of the Sustainer
increases the life of the soul.
Listen, dismiss your suspicions:
make your head a foot and hasten,
since He has bid you to come.

[V, 1666-1669]

[50] Qur'an: Surah An-Nas (Mankind), 114:1.

If continually you keep your hope
quivering like the willow in longing for Heaven,
Spiritual water and fire will continually arrive
and increase your subsistance.
And if your longing carries you there, it will be no wonder.
Don't pay attention to your weakness,
but to the intensity of your longing.
For this search is God's promise within you,
because every seeker deserves to find something of which she seeks.
Increase this search,
that your heart may escape from this bodily prison.
If your spirit shall not live without the body,
for whom is the blessing promised in the words:
in Heaven is your provision?[51]

[V, 1731-1735; 1742]

[51] Qur'an: Surah Adh-Dhariyat (The Dust Scattering Winds), 52:22.

When it comes to material food, if you eat too little,
you'll stay hungry like the crow and become angry and anemic;
if you eat your fill, you'll get indigestion.
Partake of God's food, which is easily absorbed,
and ride like a ship on the ocean of spirit.
Be patient and persistent in fasting: keep expecting God's Food.
For God, who acts with goodness and is long-suffering,
bestows His gifts on those who are hopeful.
The full-fed person doesn't wait expectantly for bread,
wondering when it might arrive;
but the one who is without food keeps asking, "Where is it?"
hungrily hopeful, that one watches for it.
Unless you are hopeful, that abundant felicity will not come to you.

[V, 1746-1753]

The foot knows its own shoe in the dark;
how should the soul not know its own body.
Dawn is a little resurrection: seeker of refuge,
judge from it what the greater resurrection will be like.
Even as the soul flies toward the clay of its body,
the scroll of every one's good and harmful actions
will fly into the left or right hand.

[V, 1779-1781]

What is the real meaning of "the inner nature of his parent"[52]?
God's creative energy is our parent:
the divine impulse is the kernel; the physical parenting is just the shell.
O nut-like body, know that Love is your friend:
inspired by Love the soul will break away the shell
in search of the kernel.

[V, 1931-1932]

What is arrogance?
It is being oblivious and insensible to what is essential,
as the ice is unaware of the sun.
When ice becomes conscious of the sun, it doesn't last long:
it warms and melts and flows away.

[V, 1941-1942]

---

[52] *Hadith*, a saying of the Prophet Muhammad.

Does anyone write something on a place
that has already been written over,
or plant a sapling where one already grows?
No; he seeks a blank piece of paper
and sows the seed where none has yet been sown.
Sister, be bare earth; be a clean piece of paper
untouched by writing, that you may be ennobled by *the pen of revelation*,[53]
so that the Gracious One may sow seed within you.

[V, 1961-1964]

If there had not been Love, how would there have been existence?
How would bread have attached itself to you and become assimilated?
The bread became you through your love and appetite;
for how else should bread have had any access to your living spirit?
Love makes lifeless bread into spirit:
it can make the spirit that was perishable everlasting.

[V, 2012-2014]

[53] Qur'an: Surah Al-Qalam (The Pen), 68, 1: *Nun wa'l Qalam* (opening words of this Surah).

In the sight of Love, fear isn't even as great as a single hair:
in the law of Love, everything is offered as a sacrifice.

[V, 2184]

Though your life has almost passed, this present moment is its root:
if it lacks moisture, water it with repentance.
Give the Living Water to the root of your life,
so that the tree of your life may flourish.
By this Water past mistakes are redeemed.
By this Water last year's poison is made sweet.

[V, 2222-2224]

The divine Mercy repaired the tattered cloak of my piety
and bestowed upon me a repentance as sweet as life.
Whatever ill deeds I had done,
It took them as not having been done;
and my undone acts of obedience
It took as having been performed.
It made me glad of heart as good fortune and felicity.
It inscribed my name in the book of the righteous:
I was one doomed to Hell;
it gave me Paradise.
When I cried, "Alas," my "Alas" became a rope,
and the rope was let down into my well.
I clutched that rope and climbed out:
I became glad and strong, sturdy, yet fragrant as a rose.
I had been lying at the bottom of a well:
now the whole world cannot contain me.
Praises be to You, O God!
You suddenly placed me far from sorrow.
Though the tip of every hair of mine should gain a tongue,
still, the thanks due to You could not be expressed.
Amid these gardens and fountains I am crying out to the people,
"*Oh, would that my people knew*!"[54]

[V, 2307-2316]

[54] Qur'an: Surah Ya Sin (O Thou Human Being), 36:26.

Trust in God is the best livelihood.
Everyone needs to trust in God
and ask, "O God, bring this work of mine to success."
Prayer involves trust in God, and trust in God
is the only means of livelihood that is independent of all others.
In these two worlds I don't know of any means of livelihood
better than trust in our Sustainer.
I know nothing better than gratitude
which brings in its wake the daily bread and its increase.

[V, 2425-2426]

Whatever is steeped in grape juice will acquire the flavor of the grape.
Whether it be carrots or apples or quinces or walnuts,
you will taste in them the delicious flavor of the grape.
When your knowledge is steeped in the light of faith,
then wayward people will receive light from it.
Whatever you say will be luminous,
for the sky never rains anything but pure water.
Become like the sky. Become like the cloud and shed rain:
the spout rains, too, but it can't produce the rain.
The water in the spout is borrowed;
the water in the cloud and sea is original.
Your thought and reasoning resemble the spout;
inspiration and revelation are like the cloud and the sky.
The rain water engenders all the colors of the garden,
while the spout causes quarrels with your neighbors.

[V, 2486-2493]

In the world there are invisible ladders,
leading step by step to the summit of heaven.
There is a different ladder for every group,
a different heaven for every path.
Each one is ignorant of the other's condition in this wide kingdom which has no end or beginning.
This one is amazed at that one and wonders why he is happy,
while that one is astonished at this one and asks why he is amazed.
God's earth is spacious[55]: every tree springs up from a certain soil.
The leaves and boughs sing thanks to God:
"What a fine, broad kingdom."
The nightingales hover around the fruiting blossom,
calling, "Give us some of what you drink."
This discourse has no end.

[V, 2556-2563]

Abruptness and haste is the Devil's wile;
patience and deliberation is God's grace.

[V, 2570]

[55] Qur'an: Surah Az-Zumar (The Throngs), 39:10.

Mountains of understanding have been submerged 818
in the seas of imagination and the whirlpools of fantasy.
Mountains are put to shame by this flood:
where is it safe except in the Ark of Noah?
By this fantasy which infests the road of Faith like a brigand,
the followers of the true Way have become split into seventy-two sects.

[V, 2654-2656]

A Shaikh would go about, with a basket in hand, saying, 819
"Give something for God's sake, if He prompts you to be generous."
His inner experiences were higher than the Footstool[56]
and the Throne[57] of God;
his outer business was to cry,
"Something for God's sake, something for God's sake!"
The prophets, every one, ply this same trade:
the people to whom they are sent are really destitute,
yet the prophets practice begging,
"Lend to God, lend to God"[58] persevering in the absurdity, "Help God!"
The shaikh goes from door to door,
while spiritually a hundred doors are open to him,
because his begging is for God's sake,
not for the sake of satisfying his own need.

[V, 2698-2703]

---

[56] Al-Kursi, the realm of the command to good and the prohibition of evil.
[57] Al-Arsh, the realm of the Divine Names.
[58] Qur'an: Surah Al-Hadid (Iron), 57:11.

The wild beast wouldn't dare to devour the flesh of the lover:
Love is recognized both by the corrupt and by the good;
and if the beast should attempt to rip the lover apart with words,
the lover's flesh will become a fatal poison.
To the beak of Love the two worlds are but a single grain.
Everything except love is devoured by Love.

[V, 2724-2726]

Serve God, so by chance you may become a lover:
devoted service is a means toward Love.
The servant desires to be freed from fate,
but God's lover wishes never to be free again.
Some servants seek benefits and robes of honor;
the lover's robe of honor is vision of the Beloved.
Not contained by speech or hearing,
Love is an ocean whose depth cannot be seen.
The drops of this Sea are innumerable:
in comparison all Seven Seas disappear.

[V, 2728-2732]

Put your hand beneath the rug, in order to fool the evil eye.
Fill your fist from beneath the rug and give the money
into the hand of the beggar whose back is broken by poverty.
From now on give from a generous wage:
give the hidden pearl to each one who desires it.
Go, be true to *the Hand of God is above their hands*[59]:
like the Hand of God, recklessly share the daily bread.
Release debtors from their debts:
like rain, make the carpet of the world green.

[V, 2792-2796]

Indeed hunger is the king of medicines:
listen, take hunger to heart, don't regard it with such contempt.
Everything unsweet is made sweet by hunger:
without hunger even delicacies have no savor.

[V, 2832-2833]

[59] Qur'an: Surah Al-Fath (Victory), 48:10.

Listen, put trust in God, don't let your hands and feet tremble with fear:
your daily bread is more in love with you than you with it.
It is in love with you and is holding back
only because it knows of your lack of self-denial.
If you had any self-denial, the daily bread
would throw itself upon you as lovers do.
What is this feverish trembling for fear of hunger?
In possession of trust in God one can live full-fed.

[V, 2851-2854]

"I am searching everywhere for a human being who is alive
with the life inspired by divine breath.
Does such a being exist?"
"This bazaar," said the other, "is crowded with human beings."
The sage answered, "I want one
who is a human being on the two-eyed road:
in the moment of anger and at the time of desire.
Where is someone who is a human being
both when anger comes and at the moment of appetite?
From street to street, I search for someone like that.
Where in the world is one who remains human in both these moments?
I would devote my life to such a human being."

[V, 2890-2894]

If you see the kettles of thought boiling:
look with intelligence on the fire, too.
God said to Job, "I have graciously bestowed
a gift of patience upon every hair of yours.
Listen, don't pay so much attention to your patience:
you've seen your patience; now look at My giving it to you.

[V, 2902-2904]

The one who regards the foam explains the mystery,
while the one who regards the Sea is bewildered.
The one who regards the foam forms intentions,
while the one who has known the Sea makes her heart one with the Sea.
The one who regards the froth calculates and reckons,
while the one who regards the Sea is without conscious volition.
The one who regards the froth is continually in motion,
while the one who regards the Sea is free of hypocrisy.

[V, 2908-2911]

If you hear a secret from a friend at midnight,
you'll know that friend when he speaks to you at dawn;
and if two people bring news to you in the night,
you'll recognize them both in the daylight by the way they speak.
If during the night the sound of a lion and the sound of a dog
enter someone's ear and he could not see them in the dark,
when day breaks and they begin to speak again,
the intelligent hearer will know them by their voice.
And so it is, that both the Devil and the angelic Spirit
present us with objects of desire
to awaken our power of choice.
There is an invisible strength within us;
when it recognizes two opposing objects of desire, it grows stronger.

[V, 3000-3005]

The interpretation of a sacred text is true
if it stirs you to hope, activity, and awe;
and if it makes you slacken your service, know the real truth to be this:
that it's a distortion of the sense of the saying, not a true interpretation.
This saying has come down to inspire you to serve—
that God may take the hands of those who have lost hope
and deliver them.
Ask the meaning of the Qur'an from the Qur'an alone,
and from that one who has set fire to his idle fancy and extinguished it,
and has become a sacrifice to the Qur'an, bowing low in humbleness,
so that the Qur'an has become the essence of his spirit.
That essential oil that has wholly devoted itself to the rose—
you can smell either that oil or the rose, as you please.

[V, 3125-3130]

Abandon being loved by people and practice loving God,
you who have such a high opinion of yourself.
You are really more silent than the night;
how long will you seek a buyer for your words?
Your hearers nod their heads in your presence,
but you waste your time in your passion to draw them near.
You say to me, "Don't be so envious,"
but how should I envy one who possesses nothing?
Instruction given to the worthless is like sketching in dust.
Instruct yourself in love of God and spiritual insight—
that endures like a pattern carved on solid stone.
Your own self is the only pupil ever really faithful to you.
All the others perish: where will you seek them, where?
While trying to make others erudite and eminent,
you are ruining yourself and draining what knowledge you have.
But when your heart is one with Reality,
you may speak, and not be afraid of becoming empty.
And so the Divine command, "*Recite!*"[60] came to the Prophet,
saying, "O righteous one, this will not fail: it is an infinite ocean."

[V, 3189-3198]

[60] Qur'an: Surah Al-Alaq (The Germ-Cell), 96:1.

The worth of a treasury is indicated by the many locks upon it.
The greatness of the traveler's goal
is marked by the intricate windings of the way,
and the mountain passes to be endured,
and the brigands infesting them.

[V, 3222-3223]

Dear soul, Love alone cuts arguments short,
for it alone comes to the rescue when you cry for help against disputes.
Eloquence is dumbfounded by Love: it dares not wrangle;
for the lover fears that, if he answers back,
the pearl of inner experience might fall out of his mouth.

[V, 3240-3241]

The companion of the Prophet said,
"Whenever the Prophet recited verses of the Qur'an to us,
at the moment of abundance that chosen Messenger
would ask attentiveness and reverence."
It's as when a bird perches on your head,
and your soul trembles for fear of its flitting,
so you don't dare to stir lest that beautiful bird take to the air;
You dare not breathe, you suppress a cough,
lest that *huma*[61] should fly away;
and should anyone speak sweet or sour words to you,
you lay a finger to your lips, meaning, "Hush!"
Bewilderment is like that bird: it makes you silent;
it puts the lid on the kettle and fills you with the boiling of love.

[V, 3244-3250]

When a spring gushes from a rock,
the rock disappears in the spring.
After that, no one calls it a "stone,"
seeing such pure water gushing forth.
Know that these bodies are vessels
valued for what God pours through them.

[V, 3283-3285]

---

[61] A mythical bird whose shadow brings blessings.

Hidden One, You who've filled the world
from East to West with Your radiance
and are exalted above the light of the Orient and the Occident,
You are the inmost Ground of Consciousness
revealing our inmost thoughts,
You are the explosive Force
that causes our damned-up rivers to surge forth.

[V, 3308-3309]

You seek knowledge from books, ridiculous!
You seek pleasure from sweets, ridiculous!
You are the sea of knowledge hidden in a dewdrop;
you are the universe hidden in a body three yards long.

[V, 3578-3579]

All this dying is not the death of the physical form:
this body is only an instrument for the spirit.
There is many a martyred soul that has died to self in this world,
though it goes about like the living.
The animal self has died, though the body, which is its sword, survives:
the sword is still in the hand of that eager warrior.
The sword is the same sword; the person is not the same person,
but this appearance of identity bewilders you.

[V, 3821; 3826-3828]

Know that the wheeling heavens are turned by waves of Love:
were it not for Love, the world would be frozen, stiff.
How would an inorganic thing transform into a plant?
How would living creatures sacrifice themselves
to become endowed with spirit?
How would the spirit sacrifice itself for the sake of that Breath
by which Mary was made pregnant?
Each one of them would be unyielding and immovable as ice:
how could they be flying and searching like locusts?
Every one is in love with that Perfection
and hastening upward like a sapling.
Their haste implicitly is saying, "Glory to God!"
They are purifying the body for the sake of the spirit.

[V, 3854-3859]

God is forever making hidden things manifest:
since they grow up, don't sow bad seed.
Rain and clouds and fire and this sun are forever
bringing up hidden things from within the earth.

[V, 3969-3970]

The spirit was made glad by that I-ness without "I"
and sprang away from the I-ness of the world.
Since it has been delivered from I, it has now become I:
blessings on the "I" that is without affliction—
for it is fleeing from its unreal I-ness
and the real I-ness is running after it,
since it saw the spirit to be selfless.
If you seek the real I-ness, it will not become a seeker of you:
only when you have died to self
will that which you seek seek you.
If you are living, how should the corpse-washer cleanse you?
If you are seeking,
how should that which you seek go in search of you?

[V, 4139-4143]

Since this house has been emptied of my furniture, 8/31
nothing great or small in the house belongs to me.
You have caused the prayer to flow forth from me like water:
give it reality accordingly and let it be granted.
You were the inspirer of the prayer in the beginning:
accordingly, be the hope for its acceptance in the end.

[V, 4161-4163]

Love has nothing to do with the five senses and the six directions:
its goal is only to experience the attraction exerted by the Beloved.
Afterwards, perhaps, permission will come from God:
the secrets that ought to be told will be told
with an eloquence nearer to the understanding
than these subtle confusing allusions.
The secret is partner with none but the knower of the secret:
in the skeptic's ear the secret is no secret at all.

[VI, 5-8]

Noah continued to call his people to God for nine hundred years,
but their denial would increase moment by moment.
Did he ever pull back the reins of speech?
Did he ever creep into the cave of silence?
He said to himself, "Does a caravan turn back from a journey
because of the barking and clamor of dogs?
On a luminous night does the outcry of dogs
delay the full moon in its course?"
The moon sheds light and the dog barks:
everyone proceeds according to his nature.

[VI, 10-14]

The four elements are four strong pillars
that support the roof of this present world.
Each pillar is a destroyer of the other:
the pillar known as water destroys the flames of fire.
The edifice of creation is based upon opposites,
and so we are always at war.
My states of mind and body are mutually opposed:
each one is opposite in its effect.
Since I am incessantly struggling with myself,
how should I act in harmony with someone else?
You cannot escape unless God saves you from this war
and brings you into the unicolored world of peace.
That world is forever flourishing,
because it's not composed of opposites.

[VI, 48-52; 55-56]

The speaker of the word
and the hearer of the word
and the words themselves—
all three become spirit in the end.

[VI, 72]

A bird flies to its nest by means of wings:
the wings of the human being are aspiration.
In the case of the lover who is soiled with good and evil,
don't pay attention to the good and evil, pay attention to the aspiration.
If a falcon is white and beyond compare,
still it becomes despicable when it hunts a mouse;
and if there is an owl that yearns for the king,
it's as noble as the falcon's head:
don't pay attention to its hood.
The human being, no bigger than a wooden kneading trough,
has surpassed in glory the heavens and the empyrean.
Did heaven ever hear the words *We have honored*[62]
which this sorrowful human being heard from God?

[VI, 134-39]

What is soul? Soul is conscious of good and evil,
rejoicing over kindness, weeping over injury.
Since consciousness is the inmost nature and essence of the soul,
the more aware you are the more spiritual you are.
Awareness is the effect of the spirit:
anyone who has this in abundance
is a man or woman of God.

[VI, 148-150]

---

[62] Qur'an: Surah Al-Isra (The Night Journey), 17:70.

Deliver me from this imprisonment of free-will,
O gracious and long-suffering Sustainer!
The one-way pull on *the straight Path*[63]
is better than the two-way pull of perplexity.
Though You are the only goal of these two ways,
still this duality is agonizing to the spirit.
Though the destination of these two ways is You alone,
still the battle is never like the banquet.
Listen to the explanation God gave in the Qur'an:
they shrank from bearing it.[64]
This perplexity in the heart is like war:
when a man is perplexed he says,
"I wonder whether this is better for my situation or that."
In perplexity the fear of failure and the hope of success
always are in conflict with each other, now advancing, now retreating.
From You came this ebb and flow within me;
otherwise, O glorious One, this sea of mine was still.
From that source from which You gave me this perplexity,
likewise now, graciously give me clarity.

[VI, 203-11]

[63] Qur'an: Surah Al-Fatihah (The Opening), 1:6.
[64] Qur'an: Surah Al-Azhab (The Confederates), 33:72.

Selfhood is a shutter
against the breeze of non-existence.

[VI, 241]

Wealth has no permanence: it comes in the morning,
and at night it is scattered to the winds.
Physical beauty too has no importance,
for a rosy face is made pale by the scratch of a single thorn.
Noble birth also is of small account,
for many become fools of money and horses.
Many a nobleman's son has disgraced his father by his wicked deeds.
Don't court a person full of talent either,
even if he seems exquisite in that respect:
take warning from the example of Iblis.
Iblis had knowledge, but since his love was not pure,
he saw in Adam nothing but a figure of clay.

[VI, 255-60]

The pleasures of this world are delightful
from a distance before the actual test.
From a distance they appear to be refreshing water,
but when you approach them, you find they are a mirage.
The world's bait is visible, but the trap is hidden:
at first sight, the world's favors seem sweet.

[VI, 316-317; 321]

God has made feeble the stratagem of liars.

[VI 352]

To follow one's own desires is to flee from God
and to spill the blood of spirituality
in the presence of His justice.

This world is a trap, and desire is its bait:
escape the traps, and quickly
turn your face towards God.

When you have followed this Way,
you have enjoyed a hundred blessings.
When you have gone the opposite way, you have fared ill.

So the Prophet said, "Consult your own hearts,
even though the religious judge
advises you about worldly affairs."

Abandon desire, and so reveal His Mercy:
you've learned by experience
the sacrifice He requires.

Since you can't escape, be His servant,
and go from His prison into His rose garden.
When you continually keep watch over your thoughts and actions,

you are always seeing the Justice and the Judge,
though heedlessness may shut your eyes,
still, that doesn't stop the sun from shining.

[VI, 377-384]

When you have eaten too much honey,
It causes you a fever, not someone else;
your day's wages aren't given to someone else at day's end.
What work have you done
without its returning to you in some form?
What seed have you sown
without the produce coming back to you?
Your own action born of your soul and body
clings to your skirt, like your own child.
In the unseen world that action
takes a form corresponding to its nature.

[VI, 417-420]

Haven't you heard the verse, *the present life is only a play*[65]?
You have squandered your goods and grown afraid.
Look for your clothes before night comes on:
don't waste the day in idle talk.

[VI, 457-458]

---

[65] Qur'an: Surah Muhammad, 47:36.

Firmness of heart is needed for achievement,
but a firm friend does not lack friends.
Be a firm friend, that you may find friends innumerable;
for without friends you will be left helpless.
Generally the wolf seizes his prey at the moment
when a year-old sheep has strayed alone from the flock.

[VI 497-498;500]

The one who cheerfully goes alone on a journey—
if he travels with companions
his progress is increased a hundredfold.
Notwithstanding the insensitivity of a donkey,
even the donkey is exhilarated, O dervish,
by comrades of its own kind
and so becomes capable of exerting strength.

To a donkey who goes alone and away from the caravan,
the road is made longer a hundredfold by fatigue.
How much more it suffers the crop and the whip
that it might cross the desert by itself!
That ass is implicitly telling you, "Pay attention!
Don't travel alone like this, unless you are an ass!"
Beyond a doubt the one who cheerfully goes alone into the toll house
proceeds more cheerfully with companions.
Every prophet on this straight path
produced the testimony of miracles and sought fellow travelers.

[VI, 512-518]

Were it not for the help of the walls,
how should houses and buildings arise?
If each wall were separate from the others,
how would the roof be held up?
Without pen and ink,
how would writing be placed on the paper?
If this rush mat were not interwoven,
the wind would carry it away.
Know that since God created pairs of every kind,
all results are produced by means of union.

[VI, 519-523]

Friends, the Beloved has blocked every escape:
we are lame deer and He a prowling lion.
Cornered by a fierce and bloodthirsty lion
what is there to do but surrender?
This Beloved, like the sun, neither sleeps nor eats:
He makes souls sleepless and hungry,
saying, "Come, be Me, or one with Me in nature,
so when I unveil Myself, you may behold My Face.
And if you had not beheld it,
how would you have become so distraught?
You were earth, and now
you long to be quickened with spiritual life."
Already the Beloved has bestowed gifts
from that world of spacelessness,
otherwise why would your spiritual eye keep gazing there?

[VI, 576-581]

The real work belongs to someone who desires God
and has severed himself from every other work.

The rest are like children who play together until it gets dark
for these few short days.

Or like someone who awakes and springs up, still drowsy,
and then is lulled back to sleep by the suggestion of an evil nurse:
"Go to sleep, my darling, I won't let anyone disturb your slumber."

If you are wise, you, yourself, will tear up your slumber by the roots,
like the thirsty man who heard the noise of the water.

God says to you, "I am the noise of the water in the ears of the thirsty;
I am rain falling from heaven.
Spring up, lover, show some excitement!
How can you hear the sound of water and then fall back asleep!"

[VI, 586-592]

Love and reputation, brother,
are not in harmony:
don't stand at the door of reputation, if you are a lover.

[VI, 612]

Should Love's heart rejoice unless I burn?
For my heart is Love's dwelling.
If You will burn Your house, burn it, Love!
Who will say, "It's not allowed"?
Burn this house thoroughly!
The lover's house improves with fire.
From now on I will make burning my aim,
for I am like the candle: burning only makes me brighter.
Abandon sleep tonight; traverse for one night
the region of the sleepless.
Look upon these lovers who have become distraught
and like moths have died in union with the One Beloved.
Look upon this ship of God's creatures
and see how it is sunk in Love.

[VI, 617-623]

In discourse, negation is used in order to affirm:
stop negating and begin affirming.
Come, stop saying, "this is not" and "that is not":
bring forward that One who has Real Being.
Put aside negation and worship only that Real Being.

[VI, 640-642]

You are my face: no wonder I don't see You:
such closeness is a mystifying veil.
You are my reason: it's no wonder I don't see You,
because of all this perplexity of thought.
You are nearer to me than my jugular vein.

[VI, 666-668]

The ship of self-consciousness, when utterly wrecked,
becomes like a sun in a bright blue sky.
Since you haven't died, your agony
has been prolonged, O candle of Tiraz!
Know that the Sun of the world is hidden if our stars can be seen.
Wield the mace against yourself; shatter your egoism to pieces,
for what you take to be "seeing" is like cotton in your ear.

[VI, 729-732]

The Messenger of good tidings said, speaking symbolically,
"Die before you die, generous ones,
even as I have died before death
and brought this reminder from Beyond."
Become the resurrection of the spirit,
so you may experience the resurrection:
this becoming is necessary for seeing and knowing
the real nature of anything.
Until you become it, you will not know it completely,
whether it be light or darkness.
If you become Reason, you will know Reason perfectly;
if you become Love, you will know Love's flaming wick.

[VI, 754-758]

Everyone in the world, whether man or woman,
is dying and continually passing through the agony of death.
Regard their words as the final injunctions
which a father gives his son.
In this way consideration and compassion may grow in your heart,
and the root of hatred and jealousy may be cut away.
Look upon your kinsman with that intention,
that your heart may burn with pity for his death agony.
Everything that is coming will come:
consider it to have already arrived;
consider your friend to already
be in the throes of death, losing his life.
If selfish motives prevent you from this insight,
cast them from your heart;
and if you cannot cast them out, don't stand inertly in incapacity:
know that with every one who feels incapable,
there is a goodly Incapacitator.
Incapacity is a chain laid upon you:
you must open your eye to behold the One who lays the chain.

[VI, 761-768]

I've paid no attention to Your warnings:
while claiming to be an idol-breaker, I've really been an idol-maker.
Should I pay more attention to Your works or to death?
Let it be death, for death is like autumn,
and You are the root from which all leaves spring.
For years death has been beating the drum,
but only when time has fled does your ear hear.
In agony the heedless man cries from the depths of his soul,
"Alas, I am dying!" Has death only just now awakened you?
Death is hoarse from shouting:
from so many astounding blows, his drum skin has split,
but you enmeshed yourself in trivialities;
and only now do you apprehend this mystery of death.

[VI, 771-776]

Does happiness reflect in your face
from the wine of the true religion?
Where is your generous hand
if you've beheld the Ocean of Abundance?
The one who sees the River doesn't grudge water to the thirsty,
especially the one who has beheld that Sea and those mighty Clouds.

[VI, 804-805]

The ant trembles and staggers with a grain of wheat,
blind to the abundance of the threshing floors.
It drags a grain along greedily and fearfully,
unaware of the stack of winnowed wheat.
The Owner of the threshing floor is calling to the ant,
"Hey, are you blind? While you have become devoted
with all your soul to that one grain,
do you really think that single grain
is all My threshing floors possess?"

[VI, 806-809]

A human being is essentially an eye;
the rest is merely flesh and skin:
whatever the eye has beheld, he is that.
A jar will submerge a mountain with its water
when the eye of the jar is open to the Sea.
When the interior of the jar has a channel to the Sea,
that jar will overwhelm a river as great as the Oxus.
In the same way whatever speech Muhammad utters,
those words are really uttered by the Sea.
All his words were pearls of the Sea,
for his heart had a passage into that Sea.
Since the bounty of the Sea is poured through our jar,
why should anyone be amazed that the Sea itself
should be contained in a Fish[66]?

[VI, 812-817]

[66] The Perfect Human Being.

Gold is the capital required for the market of this world;
in the next world, the capital is love and two eyes wet with tears.

[VI, 839]

If you want a customer who will pay in gold,
could there be a better customer than God, O my heart?
He buys our dirty bag of goods,
and in return gives us an inner light that borrows from His splendor.
He receives the dissolving ice of this mortal body
and gives a kingdom beyond imagining.
He takes a few tear drops,
and gives a spiritual spring so delicious
sugar is jealous of its sweetness.
If any doubt waylays you,
rely upon the spiritual traders, the prophets.
The Divine Ruler increased their fortune so greatly,
no mountain could bear what they've been given.

[VI, 879-882; 886-887]

If you don't see the hidden River,
see how the water wheel of stars continually turns.
If the heavens receive no rest from being moved by Love,
heart, don't ask for rest—be a circling star.

Do you think God lets you cling to any branch?
Wherever you make an attachment, He will break it.
Before God everything is like a ball,
subject to Him and prostrating before the bat.

How should you, O my heart,
being only one of a hundred billion particles,
not be in restless movement at Love's command?

[VI, 913-915; 926-927]

Read in the Surah Tin the words,
We created the Human Being in the best proportion,[67]
for the spirit is a precious pearl.
That spirit created in *the best proportion*
is beyond the range of thought.
If I declare the value of this inaccessible pearl,
both I and the hearer will be consumed.

[VI, 1005-1007]

[67] Qur'an: Surah At-Tin (The Fig), 95:4.

A disciple is like a new moon,
in reality no different than the full moon:
its apparent imperfection is a sign of gradual increase.
Night by night the newmoon gives a lesson in gradualness:
with deliberation it says, "O hasty one,
only step by step can one ascend to the roof."
A skillful cook lets the pot boil slowly;
the stew boiled in a mad hurry is of no use.

[VI, 1208-1212]

Wasn't God able to create heaven in one moment by the word "*Be*[68]"?
Without a doubt He was.
Why, then, O you who seek to be taught,
did He extend the time to six days—
every day as long as a thousand years?
Why is the creation of a child completed in nine months?
Because gradualness is a characteristic of the action of that King.

[VI, 1213-1215]

---

68 Qur'an: Surah Ya Sin (O Thou Human Being), 36:82.

With what work are you occupied,
and for what purpose are you purchased?
What sort of bird are you,
and with what digestive are you eaten?
Pass up this shop of hagglers
and seek the shop of Abundance where *God is the purchaser.*[69]
There Compassion has bought
the shabby goods no one else would look at.
With that Purchaser no base coin is rejected,
for making a profit is not the point.

[VI, 1264–1267]

Stop talking!
What a shame you have no familiarity
with inner silence!
Polish your heart for a day or two:
make that mirror your book of contemplation.

[VI, 1286–1287]

[69] Qur'an: Surah At-Tawbah (Repentance), 9:111.

Every craftsman who appeared in this world
sought a state of non-existence to demonstrate his craft.
The builder sought a ruined place where the roof had fallen in.
The water-carrier sought a pot empty of water,
a carpenter a house with no door.
At the moment of pursuing their purpose
they rush toward relative non-existence,
but then later they flee from it.
Since you have placed your hope in non-existence,
why do you turn away?
Why do you resist that which coincides with your desire?
You've torn your heart away from all you own,
you've cast the net of your heart into the sea of non-existence.
Why then do you flee this sea of the heart's desire
which has poured hundreds of thousands of fish into your net?
Why have you given the name "death"
to what is really provision for the spirit?
Observe that sorcery which makes sustenance seem like death.

[VI, 1369-1378]

Know that this troublesome body is like a coat of armor:
comfortable neither in winter nor in summer.
Yet still this bad associate is good for you
because of the patience you must show in overcoming its desires,
for the exercise of patience expands the heart with spiritual peace.
The patience shown by the moon to the dark night keeps it illumined;
the patience shown by the rose to the thorn keeps it fragrant.

[VI, 1406-1408]

Friendship is as precious as gold.
Why entrust it to one who will betray it?
Spend time near the One with whom your trusts
are safe from loss or violation.
Be close with the One who created human nature,
the One who nurtured the character of the prophets—
who if given a lamb, will give you back a whole flock of sheep.
Truly, the Sustainer cares for and increases every good quality.

[VI, 1418-1421]

The Prophet has said truly
that no one who has passed away from this world
feels sorrow, regret, or disappointment because of dying
but rather feels a hundred regrets for lost opportunities,
saying to himself, "Why didn't I keep death in mind—
death which is the storehouse of every good fortune and provision;
why, through seeing double, did I make the object of my life's attention
those fantasies that vanished at that fated hour?"
The grief of the dead isn't because of death;
no, it's because they focused on phenomenal forms
and didn't perceive that these are only the foam,
moved and fed by the Sea.

[VI, 1450-1455]

Since you have perceived the dust of forms,
perceive the wind that moves them;
since you have perceived the foam,
perceive the ocean of Creative Energy.
Come, perceive it, for in you
insight is all that matters;
the rest is just fat and flesh,
a weft and warp of bones and muscle.
Your fat never increased the light in candles;
your flesh never became roast-meat
for someone drunk with spiritual wine.
Dissolve this whole body of yours in vision:
pass into sight, pass into sight, pass into sight!
One sight perceives only two yards ahead;
another sight has beheld the two worlds
and the Face of the King.
Between these two is an incalculable difference:
seek the remedy of vision,
and God best knows that which is hidden.

[VI, 1460-1465]

Don't complain of affliction,
for it’s a smooth-paced horse
carrying you towards non-existence.

[VI, 1474]

If your thought is frozen, practice remembrance of God.
Recollection of God brings thought into movement:
make remembrance the sun for this congealed thought.

[VI, 1475-1476]

Think neither of being accepted nor of being turned away,
but always consider the Divine command and prohibition.
Then suddenly the bird of Divine attraction
will fly towards you from its nest:
as soon as you see the dawn, put out the candle.
When the eyes have become piercing,
it's the dawn's light that illumines them:
in the shell the illumined eye beholds the kernel.
In each speck it beholds the everlasting Sun;
in the drop it beholds the entire Sea.

[VI, 1479-1482]

Every shop has a different kind of merchandise:
the Mathnawi is the shop for spiritual poverty, my son.
In the shoemaker's shop there is fine leather:
if you see wood there it is only the mold for a shoe.
The drapers have silk and dun-colored cloth in their shops:
if iron is there, it's only to serve as a measuring-rod.
Our Mathnawi is the shop for Unity:
anything you see there other than the One God is just an idol.

[VI, 1525-1528]

Within tears, find a hidden laughter;
seek treasure amid ruins, sincere one.

[VI, 1586]

The Friend is your refuge and support on the Way.
If you look, you'll see the Friend is the Way.

[VI, 1592]

Carry your baggage towards silence:
when you seek the signs of the Way,
don't make yourself the focus of attention.
The Prophet said, "Know that amid the sea of cares
my Companions are like guiding stars."
Fix your eye on the stars and seek the Way;
speech confuses the sight: be silent.

[VI, 1594-1596]

If a blow comes to you from Heaven,
be alert to a gift of honor after it;
for He is not the King to slap you
without giving you a crown
and a throne on which to rest.
The whole world is worth only a gnat's wing,
but a single slap may bring an infinite reward.
Slip your neck nimbly out of this golden collar
that is the world, and take the slaps that come from God.
The prophets suffered those blows on the neck,
and from that affliction they lifted their heads high.
But always be present, attentive, and ready in yourself,
youthful one, in order that He may find you at home.
Otherwise He will take back His gift of honor,
saying, "I found no one there."

[VI, 1638-1643]

If anyone has eloquence, a listener draws it out:
the teacher's enthusiasm and energy
are derived from the child he teaches.
When the harpist who plays twenty-four musical modes
finds no ear to listen, his harp becomes a burden:
no song comes to mind; his ten fingers will not function.
If there were no ears to receive the message from the Unseen,
no prophet would have brought a Revelation from Heaven.
And if there were no eyes to see the works of God,
neither would the sky have revolved,
nor would the earth have smiled with fertile greenness.
The declaration *lawlaka*[70] means this,
that the whole business of creation
is for the sake of the perceiving eye
and the one who sees.

[VI, 1656-1661]

The cruelty of Time
and every affliction that exists
are lighter than being distant from God
and forgetful of Him.
Because afflictions will pass,
but that forgetfulness will not.
Felicity belongs only to the one
who brings his spirit near to God,
awake and mindful of Him.

[VI, 1756-1757]

---

70 "But for you," referring to the Holy Tradition (*hadith qudsi*): "But for you (O Muhammad) I would not have created the worlds."

I beg you, ask each part of yourself
to recall the bounties of the World-Provider
which are hidden in the pages of Time.
These dumb parts have a hundred tongues.

By day and by night you are eager to hear stories,
while each part of you sings of His bounties.
Like the ice which is born of winter,
when the winter disappears,
it remains as a reminder of winter's hardships.
In December a few fruit are our souvenir of summer's grace.
Similarly, my child, every single part within you
suggests the story of a bounty He bestowed.

[VI, 1794-1796; 1801-1803]

Though you read a hundred volumes without a pause,
you won't remember a single point without the Divine decree;
but if you serve God and read not a single book,
you'll learn rare sciences within your own heart.

[VI, 1931-1932]

The medicine of all intellects is just a picture of Love;
the faces of all sweethearts are but His veil.
You who are devoted to Love, turn your face towards your own face:
you have no kinsman but yourself, you who are distraught.
The fakir[71] made a qibla[72] of his heart and began to pray:
The human being has nothing but that for which he labors.[73]
Before he heard any answer to his prayer
he had been praying many years.
He prayed intently without receiving any overt response,
but in secret from Divine grace he was hearing *I am here.*[74]
Since that sickly man was always dancing without a tambourine,
in reliance upon the bounty of the Almighty Creator,
though neither a heavenly voice nor Divine messenger
was ever seen to be near,
yet the ear of his hope was filled with *Here I am.*
His hope was saying, without tongue, "Come!"
and that call was sweeping all weariness from within his heart.

[VI, 1982-1989]

---

[71] *Fakir*, literally, "a poor one."

[72] *Qibla*, the direction to which one orients in prayer.

[73] Qur'an: Surah Al-Imran (The House of Imran), 3:25.

[74] "I am here," *Labbayka*: The call of the pilgrim upon arriving at the precincts of Mecca. Here, it is God proclaiming His nearness and availability.

Patience shown to the unworthy
is the means of polishing the worthy:
wherever a heart exists, patience purifies it.

[VI, 2041]

If I had any judgment and skill of my own,
my consideration and plans would all be under my control.

At night my consciousness would not leave against my will,
and the birds of my senses
would be secured within my own cage.

I would be aware of the stages journeyed by the soul
in unconsciousness, in sleep, and in times of trouble.

But since my hand is made empty
by His sovereign power to loosen and to bind,

O, I wonder,
from whom comes this self-conceit of mine?

[VI, 2324-2327]

O, how often have knowledge and wit
become as deadly to the wayfarer as any demon or bandit!
Most of those destined for Paradise are simple-minded,
so that they escape from the mischief of philosophy.
Strip yourself of useless learning and vanity,
so that every moment Divine mercy may descend upon you.
Cleverness is the opposite of humbleness and supplication:
give up cleverness and take simplicity as your companion.
Know that cleverness is a trap for victory and ambition:
why should the pure devotee wish to be clever?
The clever are content with an ingenious device;
the simple have left all artifice
to be at rest with the Artificer,
because at breakfast time a mother will have gathered
the little child's hands and feet in repose upon her breast.

[VI, 2369-2375]

Abandon eminence and worldly energy and skill:
what matters is service to God
and a good heart.

[VI, 2500]

Since the shining truth is a cause of tranquillity,
the heart will not be calmed by lying words.
Falsehood is like a piece of straw, and the heart like a mouth:
a straw never remains quietly hidden in the mouth.
As long as it's there, the one annoyed by it keeps moving his tongue,
so that he may rid his mouth of it.

[VI, 2576-2578]

Violence is not the means of avoiding calamity:
the means is good will, tolerance, and kindness.
The Prophet said, "Alms is a means of averting calamity:
cure your diseased ones by giving alms, O youth."

[VI, 2590-2591]

What is justice? To put a thing in its right place.
What is injustice? To put a thing in its wrong place.
Nothing is vain that God has created,
whether it be anger or forbearance or sincere counsel or guile.
None of these things is absolutely good,
nor are any of them absolutely evil.
The usefulness or harm of each depends on the occasion:
for this reason knowledge is necessary and useful.
Oh, many a punishment inflicted on a poor fellow
is more meritorious than a gift of bread or sweetmeats,
for sweetmeat eaten unseasonably causes yellow bile,
whereas slaps purge him of evil.
Give the poor fellow a slap in season:
it will save him beheading later.

[VI, 2596-2602]

Take counsel with the company of the righteous:
note the Divine command given to the Prophet, "*Consult them.*"[75]
The words *their affair is a matter for consultation* are for this purpose;
through consultation mistakes and errors occur less often.
Human intellects are luminous like lamps:
twenty lamps are brighter than one.
There may happen to be among them
one lamp aflame with spiritual light,
for the jealousy of God sometimes lowers veils,
mingling the lofty with the low.
He has said, "*Travel*"[76]:
seek your fortune in the world and reap its benefits.
In all gatherings seek among minds
the kind of intellect found in the Prophet,
for the heritage of the Prophet is a consciousness
which perceives the unseen things before and after.
Amid the inward eyes, too, always be seeking that inner eye
which this Mathnawi has not the power to describe.
Hence the majestic Prophet has forbidden monasticism
and going to the mountains to live as a hermit,
in order that this kind of contact with saints should not be lost;
for to be looked upon by them is a blessing,
an elixir of eternal life.

[VI, 2611-2621]

---

[75] Qur'an: Surah Ash-Shura (Consultation) 42:38.
[76] Qur'an: Surah Al-Ankabut (The Spider), 29:20.

When Adam became the theater of Divine inspiration and love,
his rational soul revealed to him *the knowledge of the Names.*[77]
His tongue, reading from the page of his heart,
recited the name of everything that is.
Through his inward vision his tongue divulged the qualities of each;
for each it bestowed an appropriate name.
Nine hundred years Noah walked in the straight way,
and everyday he preached a new sermon.
His ruby lip drew its eloquence from the precious jewel
that is within the hearts of prophets:
he had not read Qushayri's *Risala* or the *Qutu'l-qulub* of Abu Talib.
He had not learned to preach from pouring over commentaries;
no, he learned from the fountain of revelations and the spirit—
from the wine that is so potent that when it is quaffed
the water of speech gushes from the mouth of the dumb,
and the new-born child becomes an eloquent divine
and, like the Messiah, recites words of ripened wisdom.

[VI, 2648-2656]

[77] Qur'an: Surah Al-Baqarah (The Cow), 2:29.

The ritual prayer is five times daily,
but the guide for lovers is the verse,
they who are in prayer continually.[78]
The headache of intoxication in those heads
isn't relieved by five times, nor by five hundred thousand.
"Visit once a week" is not the ration for lovers;
the soul of sincere lovers has an intense craving to drink.
"Visit once a week" is not the ration for those fish,
since they feel no spiritual joy without the Sea.

[VI, 2669-2670]

It is a sign of intimate friendship
when speech flows freely from the heart;
without intimacy, the flow is blocked.
When the heart has seen the sweetheart,
how can it remain bitter?
When a nightingale has seen the rose,
how can it keep from singing?

[VI, 2638-2639]

---

[78] Qur'an: Surah Al-Marij (The Ways of Ascent), 70:23.

If it rains during the night, no one sees the rain,
for then every soul and breath is asleep;
but the freshness of every beautiful rose garden
is clear evidence of the rain that was not seen.

[VI, 2724-2725]

Whenever a feeling of aversion comes into the heart of a good soul,
it's not without significance.
Consider that intuitive wisdom to be a Divine attribute,
not a vain suspicion:
the light of the heart has apprehended
intuitively from the Universal Tablet.

[VI, 2743-2744]

God has not created in the earth or in the lofty heaven
anything more occult than the spirit of the Human Being.
God has unfolded the mystery of all things moist or dry,
but He has sealed the mystery of the spirit:
it is of the command of God.[79]

[VI, 2877-2878]

The belly attracts bread to its resting-place;
the heat of the liver attracts water.
The eye is an attractor of beautiful persons
from these different quarters of town;
the nose is attracting scents from the garden,
while the sense of sight is an attractor of color,
and the brain and nose attract sweet perfumes.
O Lord who knows the secret, preserve us
from these attractions by the attraction of Your grace!
You, Owner of everything, are the most powerful of attractors:
it would be fitting if You would redeem the helpless.

[VI, 2901-2905]

[79] Qur'an: Surah Al-Isra (The Night Journey), 17:87.

The spirit is like an ant, and the body like a grain of wheat
which the ant carries to and fro continually.
The ant knows that the grains of which it has taken charge
will change and become assimilated.
One ant picks up a grain of barley on the road;
another ant picks up a grain of wheat and runs away.
The barley doesn't hurry to the wheat,
but the ant comes to the ant; yes it does.
The going of the barley to the wheat is merely consequential:
it's the ant that returns to its own kind.
Don't say, "Why did the wheat go to the barley?"
Fix your eye on the holder, not on that which is held.
As when a black ant moves along on a black felt cloth:
the ant is hidden from view; only the grain is visible on its way.
But Reason says, "Look well to your eye:
when does a grain ever move along without a carrier?"

[VI, 2955-2962]

11/12

Always search for the inward nature
and choose as your companion someone of good character:
Observe how rose oil has drunk the essence of the rose.
The earth of the grave is ennobled by the pure body.
Then say, "First choose the neighbor, then the house."
If you have a heart, go, seek a sweetheart.
The dust of the body is endowed with the character of the soul:
it becomes a salve for the eyes of those who are dear to God.
Many a one who sleeps like dust in the grave
is more useful and open-handed than a hundred who are still alive.
The shadow of his body has been taken away,
but his dust overshadows hundreds of thousands with his protection.

[VI, 3007-3013]

11/13

When have mice ever marched to the attack?
They have no collectedness in their souls.
Outer collectedness is futile:
listen, beg from the Creator collectedness of spirit.
Collectedness doesn't result from just gathering bodies:
know that the body, like fame, is empty as air.

[VI, 3042-3045]

11/14

Through Divine omnipotence the bodies of holy ones
have become able to support unconditioned Light.
God's power makes a glass vessel the dwelling-place
of that Light of which Sinai cannot bear even a mote.
A lamp-niche and a lamp-glass[80]
have become the dwelling-place of that Light
by which Mt. Qaf[81] and Mt. Sinai[82] are broken open.
Know that the bodies of holy ones are the lamp-niche
and their hearts the glass:
this lamp illumines the firmament.
The light of the heavens is dazzled by this Light
and vanishes like the stars in this radiance of morning.

[VI, 3066-3070]

---

[80] Qur'an: Surah An-Nur, (The Light), 14:35.
[81] The mythical mountains that surround the ends of the earth.
[82] The mountain on which Moses received the revelation of the Torah.

The Seal of the Prophets has related the saying
of the everlasting and eternal Lord:
"I am not contained in the heavens or in the void
or in the exalted intelligences and souls;
but I am contained, as a guest, in the true believer's heart,[83]
without qualification or definition or description,
so that by the mediation of that heart
everything above and below may win from Me abilities and gifts.
Without such a mirror neither earth nor time
could bear the vision of My beauty.
I caused the steed of My mercy to gallop over the two worlds.
I fashioned a spacious mirror."
From this mirror appear at every moment fifty spiritual wedding-feasts:
pay attention to the mirror, but don't ask me to describe it.

[VI, 3071-3077]

The spiritual warrior first gives away his bread;
but when the light of devotion strikes upon him,
he gives away his life.

[VI, 3086]

[83] *Hadith Qudsi*, an extra-Qur'anic revelation.

11/17

Listen, open a window to God
and begin to delight yourself
by gazing upon Him through the opening.
The business of love is to make that window in the heart,
for the breast is illumined by the beauty of the Beloved.
Gaze incessantly on the face of the Beloved!
Listen, this is in your power, my friend!

[VI, 3095-3097]

11/18

Ask of God the life of love; don't ask for the animal soul:
ask of Him that spiritual food; don't ask for bread.
Know that the world of created beings is like pure, clear water
in which the attributes of the Almighty shine.
Their knowledge, their justice, and their compassion
are like a star of heaven reflecting in running water.
Kings are the theater for the manifestation of God's kingship;
the wise are mirrors for God's wisdom.
Generations have passed away; this is a new generation:
the moon is the same moon, but the water is not the same water.
The justice is the same justice, and the learning is the same learning,
but those who came before have been supplanted.
Generations upon generations have passed away, O sovereign,
but these Divine attributes are permanent and everlasting.

[VI, 3171-3177]

When a person sees a reflection of apples in the river,
and the sight of them fills her skirt with real apples,
how should that which she saw in the river be a fantasy,
when a hundred sacks have been filled by her vision?
Don't pay attention to the body, and don't act
like those *dumb and deaf ones*
who disbelieved in Truth when it came right to them.[84]

[VI, 3194-3196]

In this ruined monastery the one who sees double
continually is moving from one corner to another,
O you who say to yourself, "The good I seek is to be found there,"
if you gain two eyes that can recognize God,
you'll see that the whole expanse of both worlds
is filled with the Beloved.

[VI, 3233-3234]

[84] Qur'an: Surah Al-Baqarah (The Cow), 2:171.

Your grace is the shepherd of all who have been created,
guarding them from the wolf of pain—
a loving shepherd like God's pen, Moses.
A single sheep fled from him: Moses wore out his shoes
and his feet blistered as he followed after it.
He continued searching until night fell;
meanwhile the flock had vanished from sight.
The lost sheep was weak and exhausted;
Moses shook the dust from it
and stroked its back and head with his hand,
fondling it lovingly like a mother.
Not a bit of irritation and anger, nothing but love and pity and tears!
He said to the sheep, "I can understand
that you naturally had no pity on me,
but why did your nature show such cruelty to itself?"
At that moment God said to the angels,
"This human being is suitable to be a prophet."

[VI, 3280-3287]

Gratitude to the benefactor is certainly the same as gratitude to God, 11/22
since it was Divine favor that caused beneficence to be bestowed.
To be ungrateful to the giver is to be ungrateful to God,
for surely his right to gratitude results from God's right.
Always give thanks to God for His bounties,
and always give thanks and praise to the Master.
Though a mother's tenderness comes from God,
still it is a sacred duty and a worthy task to serve her well.

[VI, 3254-3257]

The potter works at the pot to fashion it: 11/23
how could the pot become wide or long by itself?
The wood is kept constantly in the carpenter's hand:
how else could it be hewn and shaped properly?
The water skin is with the water carrier, skillful one,
for how else could it be filled or emptied?
Every moment you are being filled and emptied:
know then, that you are in the hand of His working.
On the day when the blindfold falls from your eye,
how madly will the work be enamored of the Maker!

[VI, 3337-3341]

The *Fatiha*[85] is unique in attracting good and averting evil.
If anything other than God appears to you,
it's the effect of His illusion;
and if all other than God vanishes from sight,
it's the effect of His awakening you to what is real.

[VI, 3355-3356]

Pure is the Builder who in the unseen world
constructs castles of speech.
Know that speech is the sound of the door
coming from the palace of mystery:
try to discern whether it is the sound of opening or closing.

The sound of the door is perceptible,
but the door itself you cannot perceive:
ye see, you are aware of the sound,
but the door *ye see not.*
When the harp of wisdom breaks into melody,
consider which way the door of the Garden of Paradise is swaying.
Since you are far from its door, pay attention to the sound.

[VI, 3481-3485]

[85] The "Opening," or first chapter of the Qur'an.

Now God causes one beautiful as the moon to appear like a nightmare,
and now He causes the bottom of a well to be delightful as a garden.
Since the closing and opening of the eye of the heart
by the Almighty is continually working lawful magic,
for this reason, Muhammad entreated God, saying,
"Let the false appear as false and the true as true,
so that in the end, when You turn the leaf,
I may not be stricken with sorrow."

[VI, 3511-3514]

I will not take back a bit of what I have given:
the milk never comes back to the teat.
According to the Prophet's saying,
the one who takes back a gift
will have become like a dog devouring his vomit.
The gifts of the sincere are never reclaimed.

[VI, 3548-3549; 3551]

11/28

O sea of bliss, O You who have stored
transcendental forms of consciousness in the heedless,
You have stored a wakefulness in sleep;
You have fastened dominion over the heart
to the state of one who has lost his heart.
You conceal riches in the lowliness of poverty;
You fasten the necklace of wealth to poverty's iron collar.
Opposite is secretly concealed in opposite:
fire is hidden within boiling water.
A delightful garden is hidden within Nimrod's fire:
income multiplies from giving and spending—
so that Muhammad, the king of prosperity, has said,
"O possessors of wealth, generosity is a gainful trade."
Riches were never diminished by alms-giving:
in truth, acts of charity
are an excellent means of increasing one's wealth.

[VI, 3567-3573]

11/29

Charity is the keeper of your purse;
the ritual prayer is the shepherd who saves you from the wolves.
The sweet fruit is hidden beneath branches and leaves:
everlasting life is hidden within death.

[VI, 3575-3576]

The peerless God has made all the six directions a theater
for the display of His signs to the clear-seeing,
so that, whatever animal or plant they look upon,
they may feed on the meadows of divine Beauty.
And so He said to the mystic companions,
"*Wherever you turn, there is the face of God.*"[86]
If in thirst you drink some water from a cup,
you are beholding God in the water.
The one who is not a lover of God
sees his own image in the water, O you of insight;
but since the lover's image has disappeared in the Beloved,
whom now should he behold in the water? Tell me that!

[VI, 3640-3645]

If there are a hundred religious books, they are but one chapter:
a hundred different religions seek but one place of worship.
All these roads end in one House:
all these thousand ears of corn are from one Seed.
All the hundred thousand sorts of food and drink
are but one thing if one looks to their final cause.
When you are entirely satiated with one kind of food,
fifty other kinds of food become displeasing to your heart.
In hunger, then, you are seeing double,
for you have regarded as more than a hundred thousand
that which is but One.

[VI, 3667-3671]

Qur'an: Surah Al-Baqarah (The Cow), 2:115.

12/2

Form is brought into existence by the Formless,
just as smoke is produced by fire.
The least blemish in the qualities of a form
annoys you when you keep looking at it;
but Formlessness absolutely bewilders you.
From non-instrumentality a hundred kinds of instruments are born.
Handlessness is fashioning hands:
the Soul of the soul shapes a complete Human Being.

[VI, 3712-3715]

12/3

Seek God in self-abasement and in self-extinction,
for nothing but forms is produced by thinking.
And if you derive no comfort except from form,
then the form that comes to birth within you involuntarily is best.
Suppose it is the form of a city to which you are going:
you are drawn there by a formless feeling of pleasure, O dependent one;
therefore, you are really going to that which has no location,
for pleasure is something different from time and place.
Suppose it is the form of a friend to whom you would go:
you are going for the sake of enjoying his company;
therefore, in reality you go to the formless world,
though you are unaware of that being the object of your journey.
In truth, then, God is worshipped by all,
since all wayfaring
is for the sake of the pleasure of which He is the source.

[VI, 3749-3755]

The prophets have conferred a great obligation on us
for they have made us aware of the end,
saying, "That which you are sowing will produce nothing but thorns;
and if you fly in this worldly direction,
you'll find there no room to fly beyond.
Get the seed from me, that it may yield a good crop;
fly with my wings, that the arrow may speed Yonder.
If you don't now recognize the necessity
and real existence of that flight to God,
in the end you'll confess it was essential."
The prophet is you, but not this unreal "you":
he is that "you" which in the end
is conscious of escape from the world of illusion.
Your last unreal "you" has come to your first real "you"
to receive admonition and gifts.
Your real "you" is buried in another unreal "you":
I am the devoted slave of one who thus sees himself.
That which the youth sees in the mirror
the Elder sees beforehand in the crude iron ingot.

[VI, 3770-3777]

The mystery of "die before death"[87] is this,
that the prizes come after dying and not before.
Except for dying,
no other skill avails with God, O artful schemer.
One Divine favor is better than a hundred kinds of personal effort:
such exertion is in danger from a hundred kinds of mischief.
And the Divine favor depends on dying:
the trustworthy authorities have put this way to the test.
No, not even the mystic's death is possible without Divine favor:
listen, listen, don't linger anywhere without Divine grace!
That grace is like an emerald, and this bodily self is an old viper:
without the emerald how should the viper be made blind?

[VI, 3837-3842]

My religion is to be kept alive by Love:
life derived from this animal soul and head alone is a disgrace.
The sword of Love sweeps away the dust from the lover's soul,
for this sword clears sins.
When the bodily dust is gone, my moon shines:
my spirit's moon finds an open sky.
For so long, O adored one, I've been beating this drum of love for you
to the tune of "See, my life depends upon my dying."

[VI, 4059-4062]

---

[87] *Hadith*, a saying of the Prophet Muhammad.

The sought and seeker are intertwined: 12/7
both the conquered and the conqueror are engaged in this sport.
This sport is not just between husband and wife:
it's the practice of everything that loves and is loved.
A mutual embracing, like that of Wis and Ramin,[88]
is Divinely ordained between eternal and non-eternal,
between substance and derivative;
but the sport is of a different character in each case:
in each instance the embracing is for a different reason.
This is said as a parable for husband and wife,
meaning, "O husband, don't dismiss your wife unkindly.
On your wedding night didn't the bridesmaid place your wife's hand
in your hand as a goodly trust?
For the evil or good which you do to her, O man worthy of confidence,
God will do the same to you.

[VI, 3950-3956]

Love is honey for the grown-up and milk for children: 12/8
for every boat it is the last weight that causes that boat to sink.

[VI, 3998]

---

[88] *Wis u Ramin*: A Persian romance.

1219 All selfish pleasures are false:
surrounding that flash of lightning is a wall of darkness.
The lightning gleams but a moment,
then surrounded by darkness, you'll find the way long.
By that light you can neither read a letter
nor ride to your destination.
But, because of your enchantment with the lightning,
the beams of sunrise withdraw from you.
Mile after mile through the night
the lightning's deception leads you,
without a guide, in a dark wilderness.

One moment you fall against a mountain, the next into a river;
now you wander in this direction, now in that.
O seeker of worldly position, you'll never find the guide;
and if you find him, you'll turn your face from him,
saying, "I've already traveled sixty miles on this road,
and now this guide tells me I've lost my way.
If I pay attention to his strange advice,
I'd have to begin my journey all over again under his orders.
I've devoted my life to this journey:
I'll pursue it come what may. Go away, O master!"

"Yes, you have journeyed far,
but only in opinion insubstantial as lightning:
come, make even a tenth of that journey
for the sake of the glorious sun of Divine inspiration.
You have read the verse, *Opinion cannot serve instead of truth*,
and yet by a lightning flash like that
you've been blinded to a rising sun.
Listen, climb into our boat, O wretched one,
or at least tie that boat of yours to this boat."

[VI, 4094-4106]

The real fortune and highway of success
lies in the business that comes to you after utter defeat.
Give up the business that has no reality:
pay attention, old donkey, get yourself a Pir![89]
May none but the Pir be your master and captain!—
not the old man of the rolling sky, Father Time,
but the Pir of right guidance.
What is required is self-surrender,
not long toil: it's useless to rush about in error.
From now on I won't seek the way to the highest heaven:
I will seek the Pir, I will seek the Pir, the Pir, the Pir!
The Pir is the ladder to Heaven:
by whom is the arrow made to fly? By the bow.

[VI, 4119-4121; 4123-4125]

I am rushing headlong: hey, let go of my feet!
Where in all my limbs is any understanding?
I am like a camel: I carry my load as long as I can,
but when I fall down exhausted, I'm glad to be killed.
If there are a hundred moats full of severed heads,
it's an absolute pleasantry in comparison with my anguish.
Nevermore in fear and dread
will I beat such a drum of passion under a blanket.
Now I will plant my banner in the open plain:
let my fate be either to lose my head
or behold the face of my Beloved!

[VI, 4164-4167]

---

[89] *Pir*, the spiritual guide.

The seeker said to himself,
"If I'd known the real nature of this being with God,
how should I have gone searching for Him?
But that knowledge depended on this journeying:
that knowing can't be gained by thinking,
no matter how precise."

[VI, 4183-4184]

You hope to earn a living as a tailor,
so that all your life you might be supported by that;
but He causes your daily bread
to come to you through the goldsmith's craft—
a means of livelihood you never imagined.
Why then, were your hopes set on tailoring,
when He didn't intend
to let your daily bread reach you from that?
It was by reason of a marvelous provision
in the knowledge of God—an order
He wrote in the eternal past:
that your thoughts should be bewildered,
so that bewilderment alone might be your business.

[VI, 4197-4201]

Inherited wealth never remains constant in the hands of its owner,
since against its will it was parted from the one who died.
Because the heir received it so easily, he doesn't know its value;
he never hastened to work and toil in order to earn it.
O so-and-so, you don't know the value of your own soul
because from His abundance, God gave it to you freely.

[VI, 4207-4209]

The Prophet has said that the true believer is like a lute
which makes music only when it's empty.
As soon as it's filled, the minstrel lays it down—
don't become full, for sweet is the touch of His hand.
Become empty and stay happily between His two fingers,
for "where" is intoxicated with the wine of "nowhere."[90]

[VI, 4213-4215]

[90] The spiritual world, which transcends all spatial relations.

12/16

The heart is comforted by true words,
just as a thirsty man is comforted by water.

[VI, 4276]

12/17

Passion makes the old medicine new:
Passion lops off the bough of weariness.
Passion is the elixir that renews:
how can there be weariness when passion is present?
Oh, don't sigh heavily from fatigue:
seek passion, seek passion, seek passion!

[VI, 4302-4304]

12/18

One day a roughneck said to a dervish,
"You're unknown to anyone here."
The dervish replied, "If the vulgar don't know me,
yet I know very well who I am."
What a pity, if the pain and spiritual illness had been reversed
and the bully had seen me as I really am,
while I was blind to myself.

[VI, 4331-4333]

What wisdom was this, that the Object of all desire
caused me to leave my home joyously on a fool's errand,
so that I was actually rushing to lose the way
and at each moment being taken farther from what I sought—
and then God in His beneficence made that very wandering
the means of my reaching the right road and finding wealth!
He makes losing the way a way to true faith;
He makes going astray a field for the harvest of righteousness,
so that no righteous one may be without fear
and no traitor may be without hope.
The Gracious One has put the antidote in the poison
so that they may say He is the Lord of hidden grace. 12/19

[VI, 4339-4344]

The business that veils me from the sight of your face 12/20
is the very essence of unemployment,
even though business may be it's name.

[VI, 4423]

12/21

Abandon this sly plotting for a while:
live free a few moments before you die.

[VI, 4444]

12/22 If the house of the head is completely filled with crazy passion,
anxiety will fill the heart.
The rest of the bodily members aren't disturbed by thinking,
but hearts are consumed by persistent thoughts.
Take refuge in the autumn gale of fear of God:
let last year's peonies be shed;
for these flowers keep new buds from blossoming,
and it's only for the sake of their growth
that the tree of the heart exists.
Put your self to sleep and escape from this vain thinking:
then lift up your head into spiritual wakefulness.
Like the Seven Sleepers of the Cave,[91] pass quickly, O mistress,
into the state of those who are *awake*
though you would say they are asleep.[92]

[VI, 4459-4464]

---

[91] A reference to the story of the Seven Men of the Cave and their miraculous sleep of several centuries. Qur'an: Surah Al Kahf (the Cave).

[92] Qur'an: Surah Al Kahf (The Cave), 18:17.

Veil the faults of others
so that veiling of your own faults
might also be granted to you.

[VI, 4526]

O body that has become the spirit's dwelling place,
enough is enough:
how long can the Sea abide in a water-skin?
O you who are a thousand Gabriel's
in the form of a human being,
O you who are many messiahs inside Jesus' donkey,
O you who are a thousand Kaabas[93]
concealed in a house of prayer,
O you who cause *'ifrit*[94] and devil to fall into error,
you are the spaceless Object of worship in space;
you destroy the devil's business,
for they say, "How should I pay homage to this clay?
How should I bestow on a mere form
a title signifying obedience?"
This human being is not form: rub your eye well,
so that you may behold in him
the radiance of the light of God's glory!

[VI, 4583-4588]

---

[93] *Kaaba*, the sacred cube structure in Mecca which is the *axis mundi* of Islamic life.
[94] Nature spirits.

12/25

The melting away of lovers
causes them to grow in spirit:
like the moon, the lover's face
shines afresh as he melts away.

[VI, 4597]

12/26

This battle of Love grows hotter each moment.
The source of its heat lies beyond the realm of space:
the seven Hells are but smoke rising from the sparks of its fire.
For this reason, O sincere one,
Hell is extinguished by Love's burning.
It says to the believer, "Pass quickly,
or my fire will be destroyed by your flames."
Behold how this breath of Love dissolves
unfaithfulness, the brimstone of Hell!
Quickly entrust your brimstone to this passion of Love,
that neither Hell nor even its sparks may assail you.
Paradise, too, says to the believer, "Pass like the breeze,
or all I possess will become unsaleable;
for you own the whole stack while I am but a gleaner:
I am but an idol, while you are the source."
Both Hell and Paradise tremble in fear of the man or woman of faith:
neither one feels safe in the presence of the truly faithful.

[VI, 4606-4614]

It's a journey on horseback as far as the sea:
after this you must have a wooden horse.
The wooden horse is useless on dry land;
it only carries those who voyage on the water.
The wooden horse is this mystical silence:
this silence instructs the seafarers.
Every such silent one who wearies you
is really uttering shrieks of love beyond.
You say, "I wonder why she is silent";
she says to herself, "How strange! Where is his ear?"

[VI, 4622-4626]

The flowers that grow from plants live but a moment;
the flowers that grow from true reason are always fresh.
Earthly flowers fade,
but the flowers that bloom from the heart—what a joy!
Know that all the delightful sciences known to us
are but two or three bouquets from that Garden.
We're devoted to these two or three
because we've shut the Garden door on ourselves.
Alas, O dear soul, that on account of your greed for bread
such admirable keys keep dropping from your hands.

[VI, 4649-4653]

12/29 God gives the things of this earth a certain color and variety and value,
causing childish folk to argue over it.
When a piece of dough is baked in the shape of a camel or lion,
these children bite their fingers excitedly in their greed.
Both lion and camel turn to bread in the mouth,
but it's futile to tell this to children.

[VI, 4717-4719]

12/30 "Tell me truly, how can you know a person's hidden nature?"
"I sit beside him in silence
and make patience a ladder to climb upwards:
patience is the key to success.
And if in his presence there should gush from my heart
words from beyond this realm of joy and sorrow,
I know that he has sent it to me from the depths of a soul
illumined like Canopus rising in Yemen."

[VI, 4912-4915]

Surely, there is a window between heart and heart. 12/31

[VI, 4916]

INDEX

A

Abundance 27, 123, 130, 143, 144, 148, 187
Adam 5, 30, 40, 45, 62, 65, 84, 99, 105, 132, 164
Angels 40, 90, 174
Anger 55, 118, 162, 174
Attention 13, 30, 33, 41, 50, 72, 75, 77, 84, 98, 99, 103, 107, 119, 130, 136, 143, 151, 155, 171, 173, 176, 184, 185

B

Beauty 40, 43, 82, 101, 132, 171, 172, 179
Beloved 12, 27, 38, 40, 47, 51, 60, 66, 71, 93, 116, 128, 137, 139, 172, 173, 179, 185
Bewilderment 8, 18, 52, 53, 65, 66, 119, 123, 125, 180, 186
Birth 35, 86, 132, 180
Body 2, 5, 10, 14, 15, 33, 35, 42, 43, 47, 63, 66, 67, 69, 73, 80, 89, 90, 94, 103, 107-109, 124, 125, 129, 135, 145, 150, 152, 168, 169, 173, 191
Breath 3, 33, 57, 58, 118, 123, 125, 166, 192

C

Candle 66, 77, 88, 90, 94, 139, 140, 152, 153
Charity 69, 98, 178
Chickpea 45
Child 24, 30, 35, 61, 70, 71, 76, 79, 81, 83, 135, 138, 147, 156, 157, 160, 164, 183, 194
Consciousness 46, 82, 109, 124, 130, 159, 163, 178
Courage 80

D

Day 5, 10, 15, 20, 26, 34, 48, 53, 60, 64, 69, 87, 95, 102, 120, 135, 138, 147, 148, 157, 164, 175, 188
Day of Reckoning 15, 26, 87
Death 21, 25, 33, 35, 39, 87, 94, 97, 100, 125, 141-143, 149, 151, 178, 182
Dervish 28, 36, 136, 188
Desire 15, 19, 41, 48, 49, 54, 83, 96, 105, 116-118, 120, 134, 138, 149, 150, 189
Despair 50
Devotion 1, 54, 94, 116, 118, 120, 144, 158, 181, 184, 193
Difficulty 16, 31, 32, 67, 79
Door 53, 54, 76, 90, 99, 104, 115, 149, 176, 193
Doubt 47, 49, 81, 136, 145, 147

E

Earth 15, 20, 29, 34, 46, 47, 69, 72, 79, 82, 98, 110, 114, 126, 137, 156, 167, 169, 171, 193, 194
Ego 41, 140
Envy 77, 121
Essence 21, 22, 26, 28, 36, 64, 81, 98, 120, 130, 169, 189
Existence 28, 34, 49, 51, 52, 55, 83, 87, 110, 180, 181

F

Face 30, 37, 39, 40, 44, 52, 98, 100, 101, 132, 134, 137, 140, 143, 152, 158, 172, 179, 184, 185, 189, 192
Faith 11, 17, 30, 57, 113, 115, 189, 192
Faithful 11, 17, 30, 46, 57, 113, 115, 189, 192
Fana 94
Fasting 91, 108
Father 65, 82, 98, 99, 132, 142, 185
Faults 25, 191

Fear 17, 21, 24, 25, 30, 33, 40, 44, 72, 80, 92, 111, 118, 122, 123, 131, 144, 185, 189, 190, 192
Felicity 10, 20, 34, 108, 112, 123, 131, 144, 185, 189, 190, 192
Fire 12, 17, 35, 43, 45, 62, 70, 85, 91, 92, 97, 107, 119, 120, 126, 129, 139, 178, 180, 192
Fool 15, 24, 60, 66, 72, 73, 90, 117, 132, 189
Form 19, 36, 45, 50, 59, 62, 82, 87, 98, 105, 119, 125, 135, 151, 152, 178, 180, 191
Free will 30, 57, 131
Friends 1, 36, 39, 40, 54, 70, 74, 102, 136, 137, 150, 165
Fragrance 8, 112, 150

G
God 1, 4, 7, 8, 11, 17-23, 29, 31-36, 42-44, 47, 48, 51-62, 64, 65, 69-71, 75-81, 84-86, 89, 90, 93, 97-100, 105-109, 112-121, 126, 128-134, 137-139, 145-148, 152-157, 160-163, 167, 169, 170, 172-182, 186-191, 194
Generosity 27, 39, 91, 106, 115, 117, 141, 143, 178
Grace 1, 7, 22, 57, 60, 85, 105, 114, 157, 158, 167, 174, 182, 189
Gratitude 27, 113, 175

H
Heart 3, 9, 13-15, 21-23, 26, 32, 36, 41, 43, 47, 49, 50, 54, 60, 62, 64, 69, 70, 74, 75, 78, 79, 84, 85, 86, 89-91, 97-99, 103, 104, 107, 112, 119, 121, 131, 134, 136, 138, 139, 142, 144, 145, 146, 148-150, 157, 158, 160, 161, 164, 165, 166, 169, 170-172, 177-179, 188, 190, 193, 195
Heaven 4, 15, 16, 31, 34, 46, 51, 82, 107, 114, 125, 130, 138, 146, 147, 155, 156, 158, 167, 170, 171, 172, 185
Home 14, 29, 86, 90, 94, 95, 101, 155, 189
Human Being 13, 30, 33, 34, 40, 48, 57, 75, 80, 87, 90, 96, 105, 118, 130, 144, 146, 150, 158, 163, 167, 174, 180, 191
Humility 103, 120, 160

I
Intelligence 30, 57, 65, 70, 83, 87, 88, 91, 119, 171
Intellect 6, 16, 20, 23, 43, 52, 66, 84, 158, 163

J
Jonah 51
Joseph 38
Journey 5, 44, 49, 64, 88, 128, 136, 159, 180, 184, 186, 192
Joy 4, 9, 32, 34, 74, 79, 165, 189, 193, 194
Jesus 24, 31, 34, 55, 78, 191
Justice 56, 104, 134, 162, 172

K
Kaaba 191
Khidr 46
Knowledge 4, 12, 28, 32, 42, 49, 66, 70, 98, 103, 113, 121, 124, 132, 160, 162, 164, 172, 186

L
Life 2, 20, 28, 32, 34, 42, 49, 66, 70, 98, 103, 113, 121, 124, 132, 160, 162, 164, 172, 186
Light 18, 19, 22, 23, 47, 52, 58, 69, 83, 86, 90, 91-93, 96, 105, 109-111, 116, 118, 121-123, 125, 128, 132, 138, 139, 141, 145, 146, 158, 164, 172, 174, 182, 183, 192, 193
Lion 21, 60, 120, 137, 194

Love 3, 4, 6, 11, 12, 28, 41, 47, 51, 52, 62, 65, 66, 72, 79, 83, 86, 90-93, 96, 105, 109, 110, 111, 116, 118, 121, 123, 125, 128, 132, 138, 139, 141, 146, 158, 164, 172, 174, 182, 183, 192, 193
the Lover 12, 28, 38, 39, 43, 47, 51, 52, 53, 93, 116, 122, 130, 138, 139, 179, 182
Luqman 2

M
Mary 1, 36, 105, 125
Men 28
Mercy 1, 7, 14, 56, 76, 106, 112, 134, 160, 171
Mirror 91, 98, 148, 171, 181
Moment 11, 21, 25, 30, 33, 34, 36, 39, 71, 72, 82, 85, 97, 100, 111, 118, 123, 128, 136, 147, 149, 160, 171, 174, 175, 184, 189, 192, 193
Moon 12, 23, 38, 95, 100, 128, 147, 150, 172, 177, 182, 192
Moses 79, 95, 174
Mother 31, 35, 79, 95, 99, 160, 174, 175
Muhammad 1, 65, 94, 96, 144, 177, 178

N
Noah 11, 60, 115, 128, 164
Non-existence 28, 34, 40, 51, 60, 94, 100, 132, 149, 153
Nothingness 51, 92, 93

O
Opposites 48, 129

P
Pain 14, 17, 31, 37, 44, 50, 54, 76, 80, 100, 105, 174, 188
Paradise 17, 19, 38, 50, 76, 82, 96, 99, 112, 160, 176, 192
Patience 3, 4, 11, 60, 98, 119, 150, 158, 194
Poverty 21, 31, 94, 95, 103, 117, 154, 178
Prayer 3, 20, 22, 34, 59, 66, 91, 98, 105, 113, 127, 158, 165, 178, 191
Pride 3, 84, 94, 95, 103, 105
Prophet 1, 12, 15, 30, 32, 41, 44, 51, 55, 60, 80, 86, 91, 94, 98, 115, 121, 123, 134, 136, 145, 150 151, 155, 156, 161, 163, 164, 171, 174, 177, 181, 187
Purity 3, 22, 41, 89, 91

Q
Qur'an 39, 45, 120, 123, 131

R
Reality 19, 23, 26, 28, 35, 54, 59, 64, 72, 121, 127, 147, 180, 185
Remembrance 40, 58, 153
Repentance 26, 76, 97, 111, 112
Resurrection 20, 82, 85, 108, 141
Righteousness 189
Rose 43, 72, 73, 74, 85, 112, 120, 134, 150, 165, 166, 169

S
Saint 23, 30, 46, 57, 163
Sea 4, 8, 10, 11, 13, 17, 22, 29, 33, 52, 63, 70, 71, 74, 77, 81, 83, 88, 90, 100, 103, 107, 109, 113, 115, 116 118, 119, 124-126, 131, 43, 144, 149, 151, 153, 155, 161, 162, 165, 167, 169, 171, 174, 178, 186, 191, 193
Search 8, 13, 22, 70, 90, 107, 109, 118, 125, 126, 169, 174, 186
Seeker 8, 13, 19, 31, 41, 42, 52, 103, 107, 108, 126, 183, 184, 186
Self 2, 8, 29, 52, 61, 80, 87, 95, 118, 121, 125, 126, 140, 159, 180, 182, 185, 190
Sema 52, 62

Senses 16, 20, 58, 128, 159
Separation 36, 47, 57, 137
Servant 17, 54, 59, 80, 84, 101, 106, 116, 134
Shaikh 60, 115
Sincerity 6, 28, 154, 162, 165, 177, 192
Solomon 13, 59
Sorrow 9, 32, 56, 79, 87, 112, 130, 151, 177, 194
Soul 16, 21-23, 26, 27, 33, 35, 39, 46, 47, 52, 55, 57-60, 70, 76, 85, 86, 91, 99, 103, 106, 108, 109, 122, 123, 125, 130, 135, 137, 143, 144, 159, 164, 165, 166, 169, 171, 172, 180, 182, 187, 193, 194
Spirit 2, 10, 12, 16, 24, 25, 30, 33, 35, 39, 40, 43, 45, 58, 62, 63, 69, 72, 74, 75, 80, 85, 90, 107, 108, 110, 120, 125, 126, 129, 130, 131, 140, 141, 146, 149, 156, 164, 167-169, 182, 191, 192

Sun 6, 37, 44, 51, 58, 75, 88, 90, 95, 101, 109, 126, 134, 137, 140, 153, 184
Sustainer 5, 89, 106, 113, 131, 150

T

Thorns 84, 104, 181
Thought 8, 13, 58, 96, 100, 113, 119, 140, 146, 153
Throne (of God) 40, 115, 155
Treasure 5, 9, 12, 24, 30, 41, 44, 51, 72, 76, 154
Trust 113, 118, 183
Truth 9, 15, 48, 57, 78, 80, 85, 87, 88, 120, 161, 173, 178, 180, 184

U

'Umar 56
Unity 76, 78, 87, 14
Universe 23, 82, 124
Unseen 16, 22, 23, 135, 156, 163, 176

V

Vision 31, 42, 62, 65, 71, 75, 82, 90, 107, 116, 149, 151, 152, 164, 171, 173, 186

W

Water 9, 10, 17, 21, 23, 24, 29, 31, 45-47, 58, 70, 74, 75, 81, 82, 85, 89, 91, 96, 97, 103, 104, 106, 107, 111, 113, 123, 127, 129, 133, 138, 143, 146, 149, 164, 167, 172, 175, 178, 179 188, 191, 193
the Way 1, 2, 6, 8, 13, 14, 17, 52, 53, 60, 75, 81, 83, 88, 106, 120, 122, 154, 155, 160, 184, 185, 189
Wealth 5, 13, 64, 98, 102, 132, 178, 187, 189
Will xii, 17, 29, 30, 50, 57, 131
Window 22, 47, 172, 195
Wings 15, 19, 26, 28, 38, 42, 46, 49, 60, 130, 181
Wisdom 6, 164, 166, 172, 176, 189
Women 48, 58, 130, 142, 192
the Word 23, 82, 85, 129, 147
Work 15, 20, 30, 48, 72, 76, 77, 85, 89, 98, 113, 135, 138, 148, 175, 187
the World 5, 10, 16, 21, 25, 28, 35, 36, 44, 48, 58, 63, 68, 74, 79, 82, 88, 89, 90, 99, 101, 114, 117, 118, 124-126, 133, 140, 142, 155, 157, 163, 172

Recommended Reading on Sufism

'Ali ibn Abi Talib. *Living and Dying with Grace: Counsels of Hadrat Ali*, translated by Thomas Cleary. Boston, 1995.

Asad, Muhammad. *The Message of the Qur'an*, Gibralter, 1984.

Bayrak, Tosun. *The Most Beautiful Names*, Putney, Vermont, 1985.

Chittick, William. *The Sufi Path of Love: The Spiritual Teachings of Rumi*, Albany, 1983.

Chittick, WIlliam. *The Sufi Path of Knowledge: Ibn al- Arabi's Metaphysics of Imagination*, Albany, 1989.

Eaton, Gai. *Islam and the Destiny of Man*. Albany, 1985.

Emre, Yunus. *The Drop That Became the Sea: Selected Lyric Poety of Yunus Emre*, translated by Refik Algan and Kabir Helminski. Putney, Vermont, 1989.

Helminski, Kabir. *Living Presence: A Sufi Way of Mindfulness & The Essential Self*. new York, 1992.

Hilmi, Ahmet. *Awakened Dreams*, translated by Refik, Algan and Camille Helminski. Putney, Vermont, 1990.

Ibn 'Arabi. *What the Seeker Needs*, translated by Bayrak and Harris. Putney, Vermont, 1992.

Rumi, Mevlâna Jalâluddin. *The Essential Rumi*, translated by Coleman Barks and John Moyne. New York, 1995.

Rumi, Mevlâna Jalâluddin. *Feeling the Shoulder of the Lion: Selected Poetry and Teaching Stories from The Mathnawi*, translated by Coleman Barks, Boston, 2000.

Rumi, Mevlâna Jalâluddin. *Love is a Stranger: Selected Lyric Poetry of Jalauddin Rumi*, translated by Kabir Helminski. Boston, 1999.

Rumi Mevlâna Jalâluddin, *Jewels of Remembrance: A Daybook of Spiritual Guidance*, translated by Camille and Kabir Helminski, Boston 2000.

Rumi, Mevlâna Jalâluddin, *The Mathnawi*, 3 vols., London, 1926

Rumi, Mevlâna Jalâluddin. *Open Secret: Versions of Rumi*, translated by Coleman Barks, Boston, 1999.

Rumi, Mevlâna Jalâluddin, *Rumi: Daylight: A Daybook of Spiritual Guidance*, translated by Camille and Kabir Helminski, Putney, Vermont, 1994.

Rumi, Mevlâna Jalâluddin. *Signs of the Unseen: Discourses of Jalaluddin Rumi* (*Fihi ma Fihi*), translated by W.M. Thackston, Jr. Putney, Vermont, 1994.

Rumi, Mevlâna Jalâluddin. *This Longing: Poetry, Teaching Stories, and Letters of Rumi*, translated by Coleman Barks and John Moyne, Putney, Vermont, 1988.

Rumi, Mevlâna Jalâluddin. *Unseen Rain: Quatrains of Rumi*, translated by Coleman Barks and John Moyne, Putney, Vermont, 1986.

Schimmel, Annemarie. *I Am Wind, You Are Fire: The Life and Work of Rumi*. Boston, 1992.

Schimmel, Annemarie. *Look This Is Love!: From the Divan of Jalaluddin Rumi*. Boston, 1990.

Schimmel, Annemarie. *Mystical Dimensions of Islam*. Chapel Hill, North Carolina, 1975.